The Last Years o:
1900

D1461177

Collins New Advanced History Series

The Last Years of Liberal England 1900-1914

K W W Aikin

Collins London and Glasgow

General Editors

K H Randell   J W Hunt

© K W W Aikin 1972

Printed in Great Britain
Collins Clear-Type Press
Set in Monotype Plantin

ISBN 0 00 327215 X

First published 1972

Contents

Full details of historical works referred to in the text will be found in the list of Further Reading on page 156. Only where the work is not included is a full reference given in the text.

Editors' foreword

The series of which this book is a part is designed to meet the needs of students in Sixth Forms and those taking courses in further and higher education. In assessing these needs two factors especially have been taken into account: the limits on the students' time which preclude the reading of all the important scholarly works, and the importance of providing stimulus to thought and imagination. Therefore the series, which has considerably more space available than even the larger single-volume textbooks on the period, presents the interpretations which have altered or increased our understanding of the age, as well as including sufficient detail to illustrate and enliven the subject. Most important of all, emphasis has been placed on discussion. Instead of outlining supposedly established facts, problems are posed as they were faced by the people of the time and as they confront the historian today in his task of interpretation. The student is thus enabled to approach the subject in an attitude of inquiry, and is encouraged to exercise his own mind on the arguments, never closed, of historiography. In so doing he will gain some knowledge of the methods of historians and of the kinds of evidence they use. He should also find enjoyment by the way.

The arrangement of the series, with several volumes covering particular aspects over a long period, and others with more strict chronological limits, has enabled each author to concentrate on an area of special interest, and should make for flexibility in use by the reader.

K.H.R.
J.W.H.

Chapter I

Unionists, Liberals and Labour

1 A new age The death of Queen Victoria on 22 January 1901 came as a great shock. The old Queen had been an impressive symbol of the stability and immortality of the age to which she had given her name. 'Censorious, insular, impetuous and sentimental, but confident in her own standard of values and in the greatness of her people, the Queen herself epitomised the weaknesses and the strengths of Victorianism'. By her dignity and sense of public duty she had increased the moral status of monarchy within the democratic framework of the constitution and had created love and respect for it among her subjects. It had undoubtedly been one of the great reigns in the history of the British monarchy, and the Queen's death seemed to mark the passing of an age.

The old Victorian order had rested on sound foundations—economic supremacy, international security and domestic harmony. However, the 1880s and 1890s brought far-reaching changes. Sir Robert Ensor captured the anxious mood of the Late Victorians when he wrote of 'the sense of an uncontrollable transition to the unknown—the feeling that the keys of power were blindly but swiftly transferring themselves to new classes, new types of men, new nations'. Foreign competition was cutting back Britain's lead in world markets. Germany's aggressive pursuit of World Power, the continued frustration of nationalist aspirations in the Balkans, and the division of European powers by the alliance system had all darkened the international situation.

Meanwhile, the advent of democracy had brought immeasurable social and political consequences to which Liberalism, which had been a magic formula for every problem in earlier days, no longer provided an answer. The formerly clear-cut objectives had gone, but as yet nothing had taken their place.

Britain's pre-eminence in the Victorian Age owed much to her economic superiority. She had been the 'workshop of the world', ideally equipped to take full advantage of the opportunities offered by free trade. Her industry had been astonishingly vigorous and her merchants had ranged the world over with her manufactured goods. Britain's trade had reached its zenith in 1870, and even as late as 1889 it had still greatly exceeded that of her two closest competitors, the U.S.A. and Germany, put together. By 1900, Britain was losing ground. Although she was still prosperous, with exports, overseas investments and her share of the world's carrying trade all rising, her long-term economic health was being severely jeopardised by increasing international competition. Not only were the populations of her main industrial rivals multiplying more rapidly than her own, but their economic growth was progressing at a faster rate, partly because they had been more willing to apply new industrial techniques. New trade patterns were emerging, and British industry was only slowly adapting to a changing world market. The export of those manufactured goods such as textiles upon which Mid-Victorian prosperity had been founded had been seriously hit from the eighties onwards by the imposition of protective tariffs by one country after another. Although new industrial factors such as electricity, oil, and the internal combustion engine were increasingly evident from the 1890s, the British economy remained unduly dependent on the established industries—textiles, steel, and coal. While these continued to grow until 1914, the conservatism of British industry postponed the sweeping technical changes and improved methods of organisation which her rivals were employing, and which would have lowered costs and increased efficiency. Britain continued to pay her way in the world, but only by exporting those goods which would ultimately benefit her rivals—machinery to equip their factories, ships that would displace British shipping, and coal, an irreplaceable natural asset.*

A new sense of uncertainty clouded Britain's world position at the end of the century. The 1890s had seen the development of threats to Britain's world-wide interests. France and Britain had been on the brink of war at Fashoda in 1898, and Russia was no less dangerous a colonial rival in Persia, Afghanistan, Tibet, and China. In 1890 Bismarck had been dismissed by his new master, William II, and his diplomatic expertise was sorely missed. Europe divided into two armed camps; Britain belonged to neither. Militant and expansionist German policies began to endanger vital British interests. The 'Kruger Telegram' (3 January 1896), encouraging Boer resistance to British expansion in South Africa, had indicated that Germany's friendship could no longer be counted on. Admiral Tirpitz, the German minister of marine, believed in creating a great German navy which would ultimately be able to dispute the supremacy of the seas with Britain. The new German Navy Laws triggered off a naval arms race which was to continue up to the outbreak of war in 1914. Germany's yearnings for 'a place in the sun', stimulated by powerful economic and military interests, impinged on British spheres of influence in the Near East and China. Britain's offers of an alliance were twice rejected. The Boer War (1899-1902) made the British government particularly aware of the dangers of isolation when international hostility coincided with military incompetence. It was not reassuring to see an army of over half a million men tied down by vastly inferior numbers of Boer guerrillas. The use of concentration camps to confine non-combatants had brought about public revulsion at such 'methods of barbarism'. 'The imperial idea', according to Professor A. P. Thornton, 'had suffered a contraction, a loss of moral content from which it never completely recovered.' (Quoted in *Edwardian England*.)

* For a fuller discussion of Britain's changing economic position, *see* T. F. May, *The Economy 1815-1914*, in this series.

While recent developments were undermining Britain's position abroad, wide-ranging political and social changes were transforming the once solid internal fabric of the Victorian state and society. The relentless progress of representative democracy was bestowing power for the first time on the underprivileged and hitherto unrepresented members of the community. The Third Reform Act (1884) and its accompanying redistribution of seats (1885) had been more radical in principle and more revolutionary in practice than either the First or Second Reform Acts. The county franchise had been democratised on the same terms as the towns had been in 1867; the electorate had been increased from three to five million. With a few exceptions, the country was divided into single-member constituencies. The democratic principle of 'one vote, one value' was established for the first time. The secret ballot (1872) and the Corrupt Practices Act (1883) had helped to break the hold of the landed classes on the counties. Not only was county electioneering transformed, but the extension of the franchise to the counties had quickened the demand for elective local authorities in the countryside, and the period 1888-99 witnessed the victory of the democratic principle in local government. Although poor men had neither the time nor the private means to sit on the new County Councils (1888), which the old ruling class continued to dominate, they were able to wield power and gain valuable experience in the arts of government on the new Parish, Urban District and Rural District Councils (1894) and on the new Metropolitan Borough Councils in London (1899). Britain was thus 'equipped for the first time with a complete modern framework for localised administration—democratic, flexible, passably honest, and capable of giving fruitful effect at the circumference to policies thought out at the national centre'.

The Liberal ethos could no longer satisfy the mass of society. Liberals had always believed that if the 'sinister interests' which prevented the free development of social and economic forces were destroyed, a natural harmony of interests would arise of its own accord. They believed in a self-regulating society in which the role of the state was reduced to a minimum. These philosophical assumptions were coming under fire by the end of the nineteenth century. The 'New Liberals' now felt that freedom within a deeply rooted social hierarchy and a developed capitalist system could only be realised by state interference, legislative intervention, collectivism and 'municipal socialism'. In the 1880s and 1890s these philosophical beliefs were as yet ill-defined and confused, but men were becoming aware of the 'labour problem'. The increased militancy and membership of the trade unions and the spread of the new socialist parties were evidence that the labouring classes were beginning to think and act for themselves. Their demands posed a major political challenge to the established parties, and it was the Conservative and Unionist party, in the ascendant between 1886 and 1902, which would appear to have wooed the working classes with the greater success.

2 The Conservative and Unionist Party   It is an interesting commentary on the average Briton's aversion to change that in the period towards the end of the nineteenth century when change was remarkably rapid, the Conservative and Unionist party had won three general elections, in 1886, 1895 and 1900, the last two with substantial majorities. These results would appear to indicate that a fundamental political swing had taken place. The Liberal party, having held office for most of the period 1832-86, was now more or less permanently in opposition. This reversal of political fortunes had stemmed primarily from the Home Rule crisis in 1886, when Gladstone had wrecked the unity of his party, accelerating the flight to the Conservatives of the propertied classes which had begun after 1867. The massive defection in 1886 of Liberal Unionists, including members from both the Whig and Radical wings of the Liberal party, had left it in a much weakened position. The Conservative and Unionist party led by Lord Salisbury now became a broad-based coalition occupying the middle ground in politics. To consolidate their numerical advantage in Parliament, the new Conservative-Liberal Unionist alliance then won popular approval by their firm rejection of Home Rule and by their pursuit of a cautiously progressive political programme which satisfied substantial sections of the enfranchised community.

Robert Blake, the historian of the Conservative party, has written that 'it is clear that the division between Liberals and Conservatives ran increasingly on lines of class and wealth towards the close of the century'. The Conservative party had traditionally been the party of the landed classes, the upper middle classes, and the Anglican Church. It had sought to maintain the ascendancy of the Crown and the House of Lords. Its main strength lay in the counties of England. In 1886, however, the Conservatives had won over the middle-class and erstwhile Liberal strongholds in the residential and commercial areas of the big cities. Since 1867 they had been gaining ever-increasing numbers of middle-class professional and business supporters, alarmed by the threat posed to established institutions and the existing social order by the democracy and demagogy of the new age. These members of the urban middle-class did not trust the new currents of radicalism that were developing within the Liberal party, particularly in its local branches. The Home Rule crisis had brought to the surface these inner tensions and had provided a favourable opportunity for a formal rejection of Liberal policies and the propagation of 'Tory Democracy', a dual conception the two meanings of which were not necessarily in conflict. While for some it meant the adoption by the Conservative party of policies designed to appeal to the new working-class voter, to others it meant giving a more democratic control over the party's organisation to the urban middle class. A relatively harmonious relationship evolved between the great territorial magnates, who continued to provide the bulk of the Party's finances, and the middle-class conservatives, who henceforth remained firmly in the Conservative and Unionist camp.

The Conservative party had also made a bid for the new working-class vote. Although it would appear that the majority of the new urban working class had voted Liberal since 1868, a significant number of them had voted Conservative since 1874 because they believed they would gain from the versions of 'Tory Democracy' preached by Disraeli, Lord Randolph Churchill and Joseph Chamberlain. A further working-class addition to the Conservative ranks had come from the cottagers and farm labourers, enfranchised for the first time in 1884. Although historical research into the 1885 election is not yet complete, it would appear that they had been attracted by the Radical programme of 'Three Acres and a Cow', and so had voted Liberal, but were subsequently alienated by Gladstone's conversion to Home Rule and neglect of social reforms. Perhaps out of deference to the traditional rulers of the countryside, they then turned to the Conservatives, who were thus able to regain control over the rural areas and country towns in 1886. Adequate funds and a permanent local party organisation enabled the Conservatives to dominate the local county associations thereafter.

The influx of the Whig landowners into the Conservative party after 1886 also strengthened its control of the counties. Whigs like Lord Hartington, however, found it difficult to join the Conservative party formally, even though there was little difference politically between them and Conservatives like Lord Salisbury, and it was Conservative votes and party organisation that would enable Liberal Unionist candidates to be returned in the future. Moreover, in order to satisfy its Whig and Radical partners in the Conservative-Liberal Unionist coalition, the Conservative party had to adopt more flexible policies. A blend of Salisburian Conservatism with Chamberlainite Radicalism was successful in keeping the party in office from 1886 till 1905, with the exception of the Liberal ministry of 1892-5.

There were many reasons for the 'Unionist Ascendancy' in these years. Lord Salisbury, Premier and Foreign Secretary since 1886, had been largely responsible for the initiation of new foreign and imperial policies that would meet the requirements of an increasingly dangerous international situation.* Uniquely qualified by his great ability and strong aristocratic connections to be a Prime Minister in the political traditions of the nineteenth

* For external affairs in this period, *see* M. C. Morgan, *Foreign Affairs 1886-1914*, in this series.

century, Salisbury saw diplomacy as the last preserve of the aristocracy. As Prime Minister he was content to delegate responsibility on domestic problems to individual ministers, while he concentrated on maintaining Britain's security in the world. Under Salisbury's direction, the Unionists were prepared to meet Germany's naval challenge by increased expenditure, and were, above all, anxious to protect and extend the British Empire. They had partly created, partly responded to the great growth of imperialist sentiment in British politics. It was Disraeli who had made imperialism an important element in Conservative policies in the 1870s. Under the cautious direction of his successor, Lord Salisbury, Britain's 'informal' Empire had been reconstituted into a 'formal' Empire in response to strategic requirements arising from swiftly changing circumstances in Europe, in Asia, and in Africa. Robinson and Gallagher have accurately described Salisbury's part in the 'Scramble for Africa'. 'Africa for him remained above all an intellectual problem, an elaborate game of bids and counterbids, of delimitations and compensations'. (*Africa and the Victorians*, Macmillan 1961.)

Joseph Chamberlain's appointment to the Colonial Office in 1895 heralded a more militant imperialism. Chamberlain believed that Britain's declining world position could be halted by the expansion and integration of her Empire. As a self-made man (he had been a very successful screw manufacturer) he particularly stressed the economic benefits of colonies as markets for British goods, as sources of raw materials for British industry, and as profitable fields for investment. Moreover, by developing the notion of 'trusteeship'—that it was Britain's moral duty to rule in order to spread Christianity and civilisation—the Unionists gave their imperialist philosophy a quasi-religious flavour. Many sections of the British electorate were caught up in enthusiasm for the 'imperial idea', particularly in the 1895 and 1900 elections, in both of which the Unionists were victorious with large majorities.

Their belief in a stronger Empire was an important factor in their opposition to Home Rule for Ireland. They refused to contemplate the division of the British Empire by granting self-government to a strategically important part of the British Isles. Their wish to continue the Union can also be explained by the fact that they were the party of the Anglican Church and of the propertied classes, and were bound therefore to maintain the Protestant ascendancy, which protected both Church and property in Ireland. By championing the rights of the Ulster Protestants, they had fortified the party's electoral position in Northern Ireland. They exploited the unpopularity of Home Rule in English politics by postponing it indefinitely. By 1900, they had succeeded in giving Ireland a decade of internal peace and comparative prosperity (*see* Chapter V).

In domestic affairs the Unionists attempted, not always successfully, to meet the needs of the time. Salisbury was a true bred-in-the-bone Conservative, and he adopted an essentially negative attitude to social reforms, being concerned only with maintaining the status quo while ameliorating conditions for the working classes wherever possible. The entry of Chamberlain and his Radical friends into the Unionist ranks after 1886 imparted a greater degree of urgency to Salisbury's approach. Chamberlain, the former Radical Mayor of Birmingham and one-time 'white hope' of the Liberal party, was the most controversial politician of the day. Blake brilliantly describes 'his ruthless determination, his harsh methods, the whiff of sulphur which hangs about so many of his actions'. His overweening ambition, political disloyalty and poor judgement had made him widely mistrusted. He may have been a maverick, but it is doubtful whether he merited Gladstone's charge: 'Chamberlain is the greatest blackguard I have ever come across.' It was Chamberlain's fate never to play the part in his country's destiny of which he thought himself capable. His chance of leading the Liberals had been lost when he parted company with Gladstone over Home Rule, and as leader of the minority group in the Conservative-Liberal Unionist coalition it was impossible for him to be either Prime Minister or Leader of the House of Commons. Although he did not hold office in a Unionist government until 1895, such was his influence that important social reforms which he advocated were passed by Salisbury's government. These reforms centred on the rural working class for two main reasons. The farm labourers and cottagers had been enfranchised in 1884, and the Unionists were anxious to have their support and thus retain power in the counties; the 'Great Depression' (1873-96) had caused more hardship in the country than in the towns and had hit those who depended on the land for their living. As a result, the Unionists provided allotments for farm labourers, facilitated cheap land transfer, altered the agricultural rating system, decreased the payments of tithe, and set up elected county, rural district and parish councils.

The long-term political future of the Unionist party might have been very much brighter had it been able to utilise more fully Chamberlain's prodigious talents, dynamic energy and far-sighted radicalism to win the support of the working classes in the towns. The Unionists did remarkably little to meet the interests of the urban working man. Social reforms such as Old Age Pensions were neglected, partly because of the Unionists' failure to make the necessary financial provision and partly because of the heavy cost of the Boer War. Working-class leaders, seeking social justice and disillusioned by the failure of both the Unionists and the Liberals to provide it, began to found their own socialist parties. According to Fraser the 'labour problem', now reinforced by a menacing ideology known as socialism, 'transformed Chamberlain the aggressive Radical into Chamberlain the defensive Unionist'. Imperialism now seemed to him an immediate and wholly acceptable alternative to socialism, which he saw as a creed appealing to the selfishness and discontent in men. As Colonial Secretary from 1895 Chamberlain became the high priest of imperialism and the strongest member of the Government, enjoying, thanks to Salisbury and Balfour, far wider powers and authority than were his due. But social reforms were indefinitely postponed.

In spite of their deficiencies, the Unionists' policies since 1886 would appear to have been vindicated by their resounding victory in the 'Khaki' election in 1900. Fighting solely on 'the waving of the flag and the cry of Khaki', they had taken electoral advantage of the general prosperity, low unemployment and patriotic sentiment induced by the Boer War. Their victory was deceptive and was due to essentially negative factors. It was the sense of national solidarity caused by the war that had rallied support to the Government of the day, rather than any widespread appeal of Unionist policies. In reality, the party had grown complacent and stale during its long period in office. Its leaders were old and tired; they had run out of ideas and were fast losing touch with what the new age required. The Liberals were too incompetent and too divided to exploit the Government's weaknesses, while the newly formed Labour Representation Committee was still in its infancy. It was hardly surprising that the Unionist party confidently expected many more years of power.

3 The Liberal Party Everything suggested that the Liberal party was well placed to take full advantage of the democratic extensions of the franchise in 1867 and 1884. As the predominant governing party since 1832, they were in a position to carry out policies which would endear them to the new working-class voters. It appears from the psephological evidence, limited though it is, that working men had indeed voted Liberal in 1868, 1880 and 1885 in the hope that the Liberals would carry out social reforms, while both the trade union movement and the 'Lib-Lab' M.P.s representing working-class constituencies were Liberal in sympathy. Yet the Liberals went on to lose the General Elections in 1886, 1895, and 1900 and seemed doomed to permanent political impotence; even when they did hold office between 1892 and 1895, they achieved little.

The Liberals' malaise stemmed primarily from the failure of the bulk of their traditional supporters, both leaders and rank-and-file, to abandon the philosophical assumptions of Liberalism. Their traditional belief that 'all the state had to do was to "hold the ring" and to ensure the conditions in which economic and political interests could have free play' can be seen in Gladstone's opposition to State intervention: 'If the Government takes into its hands that which a man ought to do for himself, it will inflict upon him greater mischiefs than all the benefits he will have received or all the advantages that would accrue from them.'

Gladstone's antipathy to the increasing collectivism of the age, his desire for the strictest economy in public expenditure, and his lack of concern for the 'condition of the people' were shared by such senior members of his party as Sir William Harcourt, John Morley, and Sir Henry Campbell-Bannerman, under whose leadership official Liberal policy continued in the hallowed Gladstonian tradition after Gladstone's departure in 1894. Laisser faire remained the central tenet of its faith. Free trade, freedom of production, stringent public economy and minimal state interference were kept in the forefront of the party's programmes. Liberal social policies thus tended to be less effective than the Unionist programme propagated by Joseph Chamberlain. Although such reforms as state regulation of factory labour, employers' liability for industrial accidents, restriction of hours of work and old age pensions were proposed by the Liberals, their approach to social reform lacked conviction. They were too limited to satisfy working-class demands, and yet were too extreme for many middle-class Liberals, who were disturbed by the extension of state intervention which such policies implied.

Moreover, as long as Gladstone had remained in political life, he had dominated the Liberal party and had uncompromisingly devoted its energies to the single issue of Home Rule for Ireland. Alan Bullock and Maurice Shock have put forward the view that justice for Ireland was the great culminating work of the Liberal tradition. 'It was only in Ireland that the sovereign Liberal remedy of Freedom had not been tried. Everywhere it had never failed, and the settlement of Ireland, the thorniest question in British politics, would be its supreme justification.' The Liberal party's moral crusade in Ireland proved politically disastrous for years to come, for not only did Home Rule split the party, but it lost votes. The Whigs saw Home Rule as yet another attack on vested interests, and they were no longer willing to make concessions. The defection of the propertied classes with their money and influence weakened the Liberal party and strengthened its Conservative opponents. The Chamberlainite Radicals likewise rebelled against Home Rule because they believed that the Liberals were pursuing a policy unpopular with the English working man, who had little love for the Irish and resented the indefinite postponement of reforms on their account. The loss of Chamberlain and his supporters was serious, for they alone might have had the imagination to produce the thorough-going social reforms which, by making the Liberal party the working man's party, would ensure its survival as a political force.

When Gladstone resigned somewhat belatedly in 1894, he left his party demoralised by a leadership struggle, beset by funda-mental disagreements on policy, and with a bleak political heritage. The party was searching for a new identity, imprisoned by its past and uncertain of what the future might hold. The Liberals' majority now depended on a combination of political, social and religious pressure groups. The 'Celtic fringe' in Ireland, Wales and Scotland, and the industrial constituencies of Northern England were now the main Liberal areas. In fact, the name 'Liberal' had come to mean different things in different parts of the country, and Liberal policies were the product of those sectional interests that gave the Liberals their majority. Indeed, the local party 'caucuses' were shaping the national policies of the Liberal party. Local party resolutions were formally adopted at the annual party conference in 1891; thus the 'New-castle programme' was a package deal of reforms, including Home Rule for the Irish, disestablishment of the Anglican Church in Wales, support for the Nonconformist School Boards in their struggle with Church Schools, and for the temperance reformers in their battle with the brewers.

However, as Sir Ivor Jennings has pointed out, 'in offering to everybody what he wanted, the Newcastle programme offered to everyone else what he did not want'. Home Rule was unpopular in England, where the settlement of substantial bodies of Irish immigrants was resented, particularly by the working class. Nonconformist and temperance demands were less effective than they had once been and antagonised the publicans, a powerful influence among the working class. 'Retrenchment' was a hope-lessly outdated cry when there was an evident need for more public expenditure and state intervention. Lords reform and 'one man, one vote' did not interest a working-class electorate that was becoming more concerned with fundamental changes in the social and economic system. The Liberals, even when in government, achieved so little for the working classes that they transferred their support elsewhere.

Foreign and colonial policies were another major factor in the decline of the Liberal party. The militant imperialism that was so popular in British politics in the last years of the century had divided the Liberals deeply. Under the idealistic leadership of Gladstone and Bright, the Liberals had sought to practise the moral principles of peace, non-intervention, and national self-determination. The heirs of this 'Little England' tradition, Harcourt and Morley, opposed the extension of the British Empire, particularly in South Africa, condemning the Boer War as 'an outrage perpetrated in the name of human freedom' and urging an immediate grant of independence to the Boer Republics. Their views were resented by an influential minority in the Liberal party, the so-called 'Liberal Imperialists', who believed in a 'forward' policy for the Empire, supported 'Chamberlain's War' wholeheartedly, and demanded the annexation of the Boer Republics. They were prepared to accept the need for diplomatic alliances and increased spending on defence in response to the growing dangers to Britain's position in the world. The activities of the Liberal Imperialists, and particularly of their leader, Lord Rosebery, seriously damaged party unity.

Rosebery, who had succeeded Gladstone as Prime Minister and party leader in 1894, must bear some of the responsibility for his party's misfortunes at this time. He was a Whig magnate and millionaire with uncommon intellectual ability and considerable personal magnetism. While anxious for political power, he was not prepared to struggle for it. His term of office as Prime Minister, while sitting in the Lords, was a failure, and he resigned as leader in 1896, his great promise unfulfilled. Returning to public life two years later, he was determined to revive his party's fortunes by a policy of imperial expansion linked to social reforms at home. He was convinced 'that only a better housed, better fed, and better educated people could fulfil its imperial destinies'. Rosebery's ideas won favour among the constituency associations and the bright young men of the party, including Asquith, Grey and Haldane, but they shook party loyalty. Disunity was a principal cause of the Liberals' poor performance in the 'Khaki Election'. Moreover, the party lacked good candidates and funds: over 160 Unionists were returned unopposed.

The year 1900 marked the nadir of the Liberals' decline. A revival followed. Sir Henry Campbell-Bannerman, the leader after 1899, was partly responsible for this recovery in his party's fortunes. Although not a politician of the first rank, he had a great fund of experience and good sense and was well liked. He belonged to the centre of the party and was concerned less with ideology than with the vital task of nursing the party back to health. His efforts were assisted by an influx of men of high calibre and by a transfusion of new ideas into the party, which thus took on a fresh look. Herbert Henry Asquith, an outstanding classical scholar, barrister and parliamentarian, had been conspicuously successful as Home Secretary in the inglorious Liberal ministry of 1892-5 and had the prospect of a bright political future. His friends on the party's Right wing, Sir Edward Grey and Richard Haldane, were two other talented juniors. David Lloyd George, the dynamic leader of the Welsh Nationalists in their demands for disestablishment and land reform, and a courageous pro-Boer, was the most prominent figure on the Liberal Left, a spokesman for the 'New Liberal' ideas of such writers as J. A. Hobson, T. H. Green and Leonard Hobhouse. Helped by the investigations of Charles Booth, Seebohm Rowntree and others into poverty and bad living conditions, they were changing the philosophical assumptions of Liberalism. The 'New Liberalism' that they produced bore witness to a social conscience, a more positive view of freedom, and a radical programme by which such liberty could be attained. They urged that the state must intervene to provide that equality of opportunity which a deeply-rooted social hierarchy and a developed capitalist system denied the individual. Hobhouse succinctly described the argument of the 'New Liberals' when he wrote: 'It is for the State to take care that the economic conditions are such that the normal man who is not defective in mind or body or will can by useful labour feed, house, and clothe himself and his family. The "right to work" and the right to a "living wage" are just as valid as the rights of person or property.' Their break with traditional Liberalism was fundamental. Here was the Liberal party's last chance to win the permanent allegiance of the working classes by implementing the social and economic reforms which the 'New Liberals' advocated. Was it already too late?

4 The emergence of the Labour Party The spread of representative democracy from 1867 onwards had to some extent liberated the working classes from their former subservience. Now that they had the vote, the key to the political future was in their hands, even though initially they seemed unaware of their power. Better education was making them more conscious of their political strength and more articulate about their grievances— long hours of work, the continual threat of unemployment, and appalling living conditions. When the Unionists and Liberals both failed to satisfy the demands of the working class, its more adventurous members decided to do something for themselves. Industrial action through the Trade Union movement was followed by a demand for political action. The decision of the Trade Union Congress in 1899 to secure Labour representation in Parliament led to the setting up of the Labour Representation Committee in 1900. This decision was perhaps the most important single factor in the growth of the Labour party.

Gladstone had partially justified the working man's trust in him and his party by supporting such important measures as his right to vote, his right to elementary education, and adequate legal status for his unions. The working classes were, however, increasingly disillusioned with the Liberals once Gladstone became preoccupied with the Irish Question and neglected the 'labour problem'. The Unionists hardly offered an alternative. Although their 'jingoism' had captured a considerable measure of working-class approval, their support for the employers, their opposition to state intervention, and their failure to pass reforms showed up 'Tory Democracy' for the sham it was. The economic depression which began in the second half of the seventies and spread into the eighties aggravated discontent amongst the poorer classes, and produced a favourable moment for the spread of socialist ideas. The socialist societies which sprang up at this time formed a second major strand in the development of the Labour party.

R. H. Tawney has defined British socialism as 'the effort, partly critical, partly constructive, at once aspiration, theory, prophecy, and programme, which has as its object to substitute for the direction of industry by the motive of personal profit and the method of unrestricted competition some principle of organisation more compatible with social solidarity and economic freedom'. It drew its inspiration from a variety of sources, some native, others continental. The Bible, as much as the ideas of Robert Owen, Ruskin, Carlyle, Henry George, Karl Marx, Frederick Engels and other collectivist writers, helped to mould Socialist thought in late Victorian Britain. Henry Pelling has emphasised the role of the socialist societies in the foundation of the Labour party. He calls them 'the one active political group interested in bringing the party into being', complete with a programme which would make it distinct and separate from the existing parties. Sir Ivor Jennings, on the other hand, has minimised the importance of socialist influence. While conceding that a few thousand socialist militants did actively propagate socialism in the trade unions and in industrial areas, he argues that 'there could have been a Labour party without the socialist societies: it is very unlikely that there could have been a Labour party without the trade unions'.

The eighties saw the first socialist societies. A wealthy Old Etonian, Henry Hyndman, founded the Democratic Federation in 1881. It became Marxist in 1883 and adopted the name of the Social Democratic Federation (S.D.F.) in 1884. It preached class war and revolution from the street corner. Its dogmatic Marxist message was incomprehensible except to little groups of middle-class intellectuals, and it had little real influence on events. As Philip Poirier observes, 'It served as a warning and example to other Socialists of what not to do.'

A more effective influence in the spread of collectivist ideas was the Fabian Society, founded in 1884. Its objective, in the words of one of its founders, was 'the reconstruction of society on a non-competitive basis with the object of remedying the evils of society'. Strong in London, it had a small and predominantly middle-class membership with only a few provincial branches and negligible working-class support. The leading Fabian personalities, George Bernard Shaw and Sidney and Beatrice Webb, did not indulge in highly original social thinking, but rather worked out practical reforms. The Fabian tracts enunciated a respectable and moderate socialist doctrine. Initially they had no intention of founding a new party, and sought to 'permeate' the Liberal party with their socialist ideas. It was only when both Liberals and Unionists failed to respond to their advice that they were forced to admit the need for a new party. It seems clear, however, that the various brands of socialism which were preached by the S.D.F. and the Fabian Society had achieved very little by 1900.

The eighties and nineties had witnessed the local growth of independent Labour parties, and three independent Labour M.P.s had been returned in 1892. The T.U.C. had decided at Glasgow in 1892 to call a conference at Bradford to form a new political party. On 13/14 January 1893, delegates from local independent Labour branches, the Scottish Labour party, trades councils, the Fabian Society, and the Social Democratic Federation founded the Independent Labour Party (I.L.P.). Henry Pelling describes the scene: 'The most interesting feature of the gathering was the presence of a new type of political delegate—the intelligent, respectable, working trade unionist of the new labour clubs. Men of this type, young and friendly, their countenances gleaming above their loose red ties, dominated the scene. They were not politicians for politics' sake; they were the working class in earnest, the product of the new education and the widening franchise. Their enthusiasm and discipline impressed the observers in the gallery and the reporters who crowded at the press table. They were tangible evidence of a new factor in British politics.'

The membership of the new party was almost entirely working-class, but its leadership, apart from Keir Hardie, was middle-class. James Keir Hardie, a self-educated Scottish miner, was the party's most outstanding figure. He had learnt his Socialism from personal experience of poverty and hardship and from the teachings of Christ, not from the economic doctrines of Marx or the class war of Hyndman. Keir Hardie had been a militant trade unionist before being elected to the Commons in 1892, where he was the 'member for the unemployed', a demagogue who sought to publicise the sufferings of the underprivileged and to sting the ruling classes into action. He, together with other I.L.P. leaders, J. Ramsay MacDonald, Bruce Glasier, Philip Snowden, and Richard Pankhurst, saw alliance with the trade union movement as their major political objective. As long as most unions remained Liberal in their politics, they would not look sympathetically towards a Socialist movement. Thus the word 'Labour' was kept in the title to identify the movement with the working class, while the word 'Socialist' was played down. The I.L.P. adopted a very flexible political programme, which was open to compromise. While the need for 'the collective ownership and control of the means of production, distribution and exchange' was tacitly acknowledged, the party emphasised those social and economic policies, such as the demand for an eight-hour day, which were most likely to appeal to the trade unions. Between 1893 and 1900, the I.L.P. sought to pursue a middle course of 'Independence', leaning in the direction neither of the Socialists nor of the Liberals.

The years 1895 to 1900 were a particularly difficult time for the new party. The I.L.P. candidates were heavily defeated in the by-elections they contested, and in the 1895 General Election, when even Keir Hardie lost his seat. Membership was declining, funds were short, and the political apathy of the working classes was proving insuperable. 'The difficulty in England', the Fabians complained in 1896, 'is not to secure more political power for the people, but to persuade them to make any sensible use of the power they already have.' The only ray of hope came from the increasing number of I.L.P. members elected to the new local councils, where they were able to gain invaluable political and administrative experience, and from the mounting insecurity of the trade union movement in the late 1890s.

The trade union movement had traditionally been non-militant, respectable and exclusive, representing the older 'craft' unions of skilled workers. Conscious of their financial weakness and their vulnerability in the law courts, the trade unions were gradually establishing themselves as a typically responsible English institution. The use of trade unions as pressure groups was more practicable once the urban working class had been given the vote in 1867. In 1871 the T.U.C. appointed a Parliamentary Committee to lobby for the full recognition of trade union rights. The trade unions were generally Liberal in sympathy, although important unions like the Lancashire cotton operatives were Conservative. This link with Liberalism can be explained in several ways. The close ties between Liberalism, Nonconformity and the temperance reformers attracted many respectable trade unionists, who were regular chapel-goers and teetotallers. Some mining constituency parties had fallen under the control of politically active working men, and working-class candidates, financed by their unions, were nominated and returned as Liberals. The first two 'Lib-Labs', as these working men were called, were elected to Parliament in 1874, where they accepted the Liberal whip and were indistinguishable from members of the official Liberal party. Elsewhere, the middle classes continued to dominate the local Liberal associations in industrial areas and to nominate middle-class candidates with independent means; working men could not support themselves financially and were not put forward.

The older trade unions had represented skilled workers; the manual or semi-skilled workers had not been organised into unions. By 1888, only about 750,000 workers belonged to trade unions. Suffering the effects of the slump and impatient with their lowly status, the unskilled working class began to take industrial action to achieve their objectives. London match-girls, gas workers and dockers all went on strike in 1888-9 for higher wages and shorter working hours. The success of their strikes helped to bring about a remarkable rise in union membership: not only did the older unions gain more members, but 'new unions' for the unskilled and poorly paid workers were founded. Membership rose to 1,576,000 by 1892 and topped the two million mark by 1900. The 'new unions' were more class-conscious and more susceptible to socialist ideas than the older ones, and many union officials belonged to the various socialist societies. It was this novel connection between the trade unions and the socialists that was perhaps the most decisive stimulus to the emergence of a Labour party.

The dramatic increase in trade union membership and the strident militancy of the 'new unions' had contributed to a deterioration in relations with management. The development of large combinations in place of private firms had made collective bargaining more impersonal and less profitable. The employers' attitudes had hardened. A showdown between management and unions seemed imminent. In 1893, the National Free Labour Association had been founded to supply 'free' labour to take the place of strikers; such 'blacklegs' only increased bitterness and prolonged strikes. In July 1897, the Amalgamated Society of Engineers, the most powerful union in the country, had gone on strike in London for an eight-hour day. The Employers' Federation of Engineering Associations, founded in 1896, determined to meet strength with strength and ordered a national lock-out. The A.S.E. finally succumbed in January 1898 to the employers' terms, its strike fund depleted by the considerable sum of £489,000.

An attack on the trade unions was at the same time being mounted in Parliament and in the law courts. In 1898, the Employers' Parliamentary Council was set up to promote the interests of the employers; Unionist M.P.s were immediately sympathetic to this influential lobby, which demanded a stricter interpretation of the law concerning intimidation and picketing. Meanwhile, the confidence of the trade unions in their legal position was being eroded by the decisions in a number of important lawsuits on such vital matters as the unions' liability for damages. The case of *Lyons v. Wilkins* (1896-8) seemed to place a severe restriction on the right of peaceful picketing; if the unions could not picket, they would lose their major weapon in effectively carrying on a strike. Trade union leaders now began to doubt whether industrial action was, in fact, proving more effective than political action through Parliament. They felt that, with strikes too expensive, fair treatment under the law unobtainable, and clarification of the trade union laws unlikely in the Unionist-dominated Parliament, they must increase the 'Labour' representation in the Commons. A resolution was passed by 546,000 votes to 434,000 votes at the Trade Unions' Plymouth Congress in September 1899 that a special conference to discuss Labour representation be held.

The conference opened in London on 27 February 1900, and attendance was voluntary. One hundred and twenty-nine delegates from the I.L.P., the Fabian Society, the S.D.F., and the trade unions took part; over two-thirds of the unions belonging to the T.U.C. did not attend. The conference agreed to set up a distinct Labour group in the House of Commons which would support measures in favour of Labour and would oppose hostile legislation. A Labour Representation Committee (L.R.C.) was appointed, financed by an annual levy on each affiliated society of 10/- for each 1000 members. It was to call an annual conference, keep in touch with the trade unions, and publish a list of L.R.C.-sponsored candidates at election time whose expenses would be met by the separate organisations belonging to the L.R.C. The importance of the L.R.C. lay in the fact that socialists and trade unionists had for the first time met on common ground and had consented to support parliamentary candidates sympathetic to the 'Labour' point of view. This 'Great Alliance' was a major landmark in the history of the Labour movement.

The L.R.C. was primarily a compromise arrangement designed to accommodate as many disparate elements as possible (S.D.F., I.L.P., trade union Liberals, 'Lib-Labs', Fabians) under the same roof. The L.R.C.'s leaders therefore had to steer a difficult middle course between the doctrinaire socialism of the S.D.F. and the conventional liberalism of most trade unionists. While the older men, Keir Hardie and Bruce Glasier, kept alive the socialist ideals of the Labour movement, the dominant influence over L.R.C. policy was exerted by its young Secretary, Ramsay MacDonald. Of humble Scottish origins and illegitimate, he had educated himself and had become a journalist in London. Immersing himself in left-wing politics, he had belonged to the S.D.F. and the Fabians before joining the I.L.P. MacDonald was a first-class politician, whose opportunism, powers of organisation, realism, and willingness to compromise enabled the L.R.C. to survive a difficult political beginning. Not only did he play a crucial role in the foundation and organisation of the new political party, but he gave that party an all-embracing, evolutionary creed of socialism which was in harmony with the anti-revolutionary temper of the average working man. MacDonald believed that 'each new stage in evolution retains all that was vital in the old and sheds all that was dead . . . Socialism, the stage which follows Liberalism, retains everything of permanent value that was in Liberalism by virtue of its being the hereditary heir of Liberalism.' Such moderate views were too much for the S.D.F., which seceded from the L.R.C. in 1901, but MacDonald's carefully calculated tactics of emphasising the similarities with the Liberal programme, and yet showing the independent political stance of the new Labour party made good political sense. MacDonald was, in effect, prepared to sacrifice an out-and-out socialist programme until the day when there was a strong and permanent Labour voice in the Commons.

The 'Khaki' election in October 1900 caught the new party totally unprepared. Labour supporters were divided in their attitudes to the Boer War, only limited funds were available, and insufficient groundwork had been done for the L.R.C. to expect much success. MacDonald himself was in South Africa when the election was called. Many Government-held seats which might have fallen were not captured because the lack of a proper understanding between the L.R.C. and the Liberals split the anti-Government vote. In a total of 15 contests, the L.R.C. had polled 62,698 out of some 170,000 votes, and had elected two M.P.s, Keir Hardie and Richard Bell. The foundation of a permanent working-class political organisation had been laid.

Chapter II

The Fall of the Unionists 1900-6

1 The Education Act 1902 The Unionists had won the 1900 election on false pretences, for, taking full advantage of the prevailing mood of patriotism, Salisbury and his supporters had offered little in the way of new policies. In fact the old and ailing Premier was more a respected figurehead than an effective force in the government. In 1900 he was persuaded to hand over the Foreign Office to Lord Landsowne, and in 1902, when he resigned the premiership, having been Prime Minister for a total of thirteen and a half years, he was succeeded with the minimum of difficulty by his nephew Arthur Balfour. A highly intelligent and wealthy aristocrat, Balfour had the political world at his feet. Although a born Conservative, he accepted realistically that change was bound to come. He had been a successful Chief Secretary in Ireland between 1887 and 1891, and since then had led the Unionist party in the Commons. Cool and unruffled, a ruthless debater and a skilful politician, he has been compared with 'a powerful graceful cat walking delicately and unsoiled across a rather muddy street'. Winston Churchill went on to say that 'had his life been cast amid the labyrinthine intrigues of the Italian Renaissance, he would not have required to study the works of Machiavelli'. Balfour achieved much success in his ministry in matters of education, defence, and foreign policy, but various personal defects made him a bad leader. His hobby was philosophy. 'Shivering in philosophic doubt on the steps of a metaphysical bathing machine', he projected an image of uncertainty, incapable of giving a clear and decisive lead. His aloofness from the man in the street was a further handicap. As Robert Blake observes, 'The truth was that he was too rational and that he made insufficient allowance for the unreason of the masses.' Thus, on the level of practical politics, Balfour had blind spots, and this was to be a major reason for the failure of his ministry. His Cabinet was not an inspiring one: good men were hard to find, and it was difficult to give the Government a new look.

The political situation had changed since 1900. The high moral tone of imperialism had been discredited by the methods used to bring victory over the Boers, while Campbell-Bannerman, in denouncing those same methods, had partly succeeded in reuniting the Liberal factions. While the war lasted, it had deflected public interest from domestic politics; the Conservatives, as the patriotic party, had benefited. However, the signing of the Peace of Vereeniging on 31 May 1902 helped to revive interest in home affairs, and political opinion, as far as it can be assessed, began to veer towards the Left. The Government accelerated the change of mood between 1902 and 1905 by a series of controversial measures and major mistakes, and consequently helped to bring a truly calamitous defeat upon themselves in the 1906 election.

The Education Act of 1902 was the first important setback. It was a good example both of Balfour's constructive statesmanship and his blindness to public opinion. He was aware that Britain's survival as a great Power would to some extent rest on the quality of her educational system, and it was this that was causing concern to many politicians and educationalists. Forster's Education Act (1870) had for the first time brought elementary schools within the reach of every child, and had set up popularly elected boards to run the new schools. An enormous expansion of educational institutions had resulted. By concentrating on the 'three Rs', the battle against mere illiteracy was won. Equally encouraging progress was being made in the education of women and in the expansion of university education. By the turn of the century, secondary education was the problem. A haphazard and ill-co-ordinated system had grown up. Some board schools had taken to providing more advanced courses, others evening classes for their senior pupils who stayed on at school until fourteen. Elsewhere the public schools and old endowed grammar schools provided a more academic type of secondary education. Then, in 1889, the Technical Instruction Act, by setting up a local authority for technical education (the county, or county borough, council) had added to the overlapping agencies providing secondary education. The Bryce Commission was appointed in 1894 to investigate ways of remedying the defects in the system, and recommended a reorganisation of the existing situation by fitting the educational authorities into the new structure of local government. Nothing had been done before 1902 to implement this proposal.

R. L. Morant, an official at the Board of Education, had served on the Commission and was prominent in urging action upon the Government. He was able to work closely with Balfour, who, according to his niece and biographer, Lady Blanche Dugdale, 'never inspired a deeper devotion in a subordinate and the zeal of another never had more influence on himself'. Morant was hostile to the school boards. He had discovered in 1898 that they were exceeding their statutory powers in providing secondary education and that their activities could be stopped by law. He was instrumental, therefore, in bringing a test case against them. In 1899, the official auditor, T. B. Cockerton, indicted the London School Board as personally liable for several items of illegal expenditure. If the indictment was upheld, it would destroy the legal basis of higher education as practised in hundreds of day and evening schools throughout the country. Cockerton won his case in both the Court of Queen's Bench (1900) and the Court of Appeal (1901): the judgement was a condemnation of all the Board's higher grade and evening school work. A one-clause Act was passed to legalise the schools for a year only, making a new and permanent solution essential.

The question of education was, however, complicated by important religious and political considerations. Neither party could introduce reforms without antagonising some sectional interests. Anglicans, who had traditionally looked to the Conservatives for support, pressed for Government aid to church schools, which were in considerable financial difficulty. Noncon-formists, who generally relied on the Liberal party to represent their interests, were on the other hand hoping that the church schools, which they regarded as rivals to the board schools, would be forced to close because of their financial weakness. They had gained control of the school boards since 1870, and it was clear that they and many Liberal Unionists would revolt against any attempt to strengthen Anglican influences in educa-tion. Balfour's attitude has provoked some difference of opinion among historians. Why, when party unity meant so much to him and when he was forewarned that the Bill would strain party loyalties and ultimately lead to defeat, did he press the 1902 Education Act at all? His biographer, Kenneth Young, gener-ously emphasises Balfour's willingness to face up to the challenge in the national interest, even though the cost in political terms would be great, whereas Peter Fraser argues that Balfour had no real choice but to pass the Act. Robert Blake, however, while recognising its value, uses the Act as conclusive evidence of Balfour's myopia, of his failure to foresee the unpopularity that the measure would arouse.

In March 1902, Balfour himself introduced the Education Bill into the Commons, and on 20 December it became law. For the first time in England, the provision of secondary education was recognised as the duty of the state and was brought under public control. The Bill provided a unified educational system covering elementary and secondary education. Only the London School Board was to survive the abolition of school boards throughout the country, and that for only a year. The councils of the counties and county boroughs were made the local edu-cation authorities, with the exception that non-county boroughs with a population of over 10,000 and urban districts with a population of over 20,000 were to be responsible for ele-mentary education in their areas. Voluntary (i.e. Church) schools, in return for providing the school buildings, were to retain their right to appoint teachers and were to receive funds from local rates to meet their current expenses. Not only would this satisfy the demands of the church schools, Anglican and Catholic, for financial support, but for the first time public money would be available to ensure adequate pay for teachers and a uniform standard of efficiency for all children. 'Undenominational' teaching, which the Nonconformists preferred, was retained in the 'provided' or state schools by the Cowper-Temple clause of the Bill. The new local education authorities (L.E.A.s) were to operate by means of a statutory education committee which could include members co-opted from outside the council. Lord Londonderry was appointed first President of the Board of Education, with Morant, hitherto a junior official, as head of the department.

The Act was one of the great constructive reforms of the twentieth century and remained the basis of secondary education in England and Wales until 1944. There was a rapid increase in the number of secondary schools after the acts of 1902 and (for London) 1903. New schools were built, and some old board schools developed as 'central' schools of a higher-education type. Many historic grammar schools also came under the L.E.A.s. There was now a conjunction between elementary and secondary schools where previously there had been two separate systems. The great extension of scholarships and free places by the Liberals after 1906 had the effect of tapping a wider range of ability. The number of pupils in grant-aided secondary schools had risen from 94,000 in 1905 to about 200,000 at the outbreak of war. Increased government spending on education had undoubtedly helped to raise the general standard. The large demand for well-qualified people was being met, more than justifying the hopes of Balfour, Morant, and other educational reformers.

As had been predicted, however, the Education Act caused a political furore which severely damaged the Government's standing in the country. Nonconformists in particular objected to the principle of sectarian schools being supported by the rates, even though the same schools had for some time been drawing government grants. They now had to watch the hated church schools being rescued by public funds and their beloved school boards abolished. They particularly resented the existence of many 'single school' areas, such as rural Wales, where the only school was a church school and Nonconformist children had no alternative but to attend it. The Unionist party was split along the line which separated Anglicans and Nonconformists; many Nonconformists among the Liberal Unionists now returned to the Liberal fold. Joseph Chamberlain wrote gloomily to the Duke of Devonshire in September 1902: 'I told you that your Education Bill would destroy your own party. It has done so. Our best friends are leaving us by scores and hundreds, and they will not come back'. The Nonconformists' fervent denunciation of the Bill both in and out of Parliament could not help but revive the morale and political effectiveness of the Liberal party. They continued to protest after it had become law. Dr. John Clifford, a much respected Baptist, and the National Council of the Free Churches directed the agitation. A campaign of passive resistance was launched against the payment of the education rate, and over 7000 summonses had to be issued for non-payment. In Wales, certain councils refused to carry out their statutory duties. Above all, the Nonconformists determined to strive for the repeal of the Act by ensuring a Liberal victory at the next election. They worked to increase their representation in Parliament, and by fighting by-elections helped to reduce support for the Government and paved the way for future Liberal success. There can be little doubt that the momentum from this Nonconformist crusade played a significant part in the Liberal revival.

2 Tariff reform 1903-5   Joseph Chamberlain, who had helped to wreck the unity of the Liberal party in 1886, ended his political career by destroying the unity of the Conservative and Unionist party and ensuring its defeat in the 1906 election. Frustrated by the rapid waning of Unionist fortunes after the struggle over education, Chamberlain sought to galvanise the Unionist party with a new cause. His Birmingham speech in May 1903, announcing his rejection of free trade, his belief in imperial preference and his desire for fiscal retaliation against foreign tariffs (Tariff Reform) was later described by one of his young admirers, L. S.

Amery, as 'a challenge to free trade as direct and provocative as the theses which Luther nailed to the church door at Wittenberg'. It caused a political sensation. No other issue, either during Balfour's term of office or for many years after, was to do so much damage to the electoral prospects of the Unionist party.

What Chamberlain wanted, according to Robert Blake, was 'political unity in the form of imperial federation, economic unity in the form of a customs union, military unity in the form of the integration of the colonial forces'. Moreover, Chamberlain believed in social reform as the best hope of warding off the rising challenge of socialism and winning working-class voters to Conservatism. His long-standing plans to introduce old age pensions had been continually frustrated by the reluctance of the Chancellor of the Exchequer, Hicks Beach, who was firmly wedded to the Gladstonian ideal of 'retrenchment', to provide the necessary funds. The increased expenditure incurred during the Boer War was met from old sources of revenue and by economy in its traditional form—social reform was postponed indefinitely. Passionately believing in the Empire, Chamberlain had ceaselessly laboured for closer Imperial unity. He shared the opinion of the six 'self-governing' colonies, which had attended the Fourth Colonial Conference in London in July-August, 1902, that the British Government should adopt the principle of imperial preference in regard to trade. The new fiscal policy of protection would in Chamberlain's view provide the necessary revenue for social reform. Tariff Reform was thus a vision which would link the two causes of empire and social reconstruction, and benefit the British economy at the same time. The belief in free trade, which prevailed among all parties and all classes, was the major stumbling-block to Chamberlain's schemes. Professor Asa Briggs has written, 'For some . . . free trade was still a religion. The principles behind it were eternal: its revelation was the greatest triumph of the nineteenth century.' Yet this was the very shibboleth that Chamberlain determined to challenge.

Economic arguments for and against Tariff Reform were prominent in the nation-wide debate that followed Chamberlain's action. The question was: did Britain's present economic situation justify protection? Although it has been shown elsewhere that Britain's overall trading position was declining in relation to her major rivals, it was not clear whether the volume and competition of foreign goods had progressed far enough to justify protection. It was difficult in 1903 to obtain a general picture of the economy; some industries (metal manufactures, glass, chemicals, building materials) would certainly benefit from protection, others would not. While there was an economic recession between 1901 and 1903 when Britain was suffering from foreign competition and 'dumping', 1903-5 saw rising exports, increased investments overseas, higher 'invisible' earnings, and sufficient prosperity to justify the retention of free trade and an optimistic view of the future. The free trade lobby pointed out how 1903-5 had shown a far more rapid expansion in exports to foreign countries than to the colonies, and argued that protection would add to the costs of production by making factory plant and raw materials more expensive. They claimed that protection would force up food prices and that wages would in turn have to rise; thus the costs of production would rise still further and consequently British goods would be made less competitive in world markets.*

A more damaging argument used against the tariff reformers was that the undoubted rise in food prices that would follow the imposition of tariffs would for the general public outweigh the benefits of protection. The free traders seized on the symbolism of the 'big' and the 'small' loaf, which had been so effective in the struggle for free trade in the 'Hungry Forties'. Their appeal for cheap food and no 'stomach taxes' aroused a far greater response from the working class than Chamberlain's claim that the Empire served working-class interests, and that Tariff Reform would prepare the way for more jobs and more social reforms. Chamberlain, alas, had lost his old working-class audience. They were no longer listening to his promises of social reform, while their belief in the Empire had been shaken by the

* For the economic history of this period, see T. F. May, *The Economy 1815-1914*, in this series.

stories of the 'concentration camps' and 'Chinese Slavery' in South Africa. With unemployment high in 1904-5 and Unionist remedies inadequate, Chamberlain's bid to win the working classes to conservatism was hopelessly ill-timed. Tariff Reform, in fact, completed the alienation of the majority of working-class voters from the Unionist party.

The Tariff Reform issue had its immediate origins in 1902, when the Boer War had caused a deficit for which Hicks Beach found additional revenue by imposing a 'registration' duty of one shilling on imported corn and flour, thus reviving a tax that had been abolished in 1869. This duty had only a symbolic importance, but both protectionists and free traders thought not of what it was, but of where it might lead. While Chamberlain was thinking that the corn duty might be a first step towards imperial preference, protests from free traders were so strong that Balfour's party agent reported that the corn duty was proving more harmful electorally than the education issue. Just before Chamberlain left on a visit to South Africa at the end of 1902, a Cabinet meeting decided that 'they would maintain the corn-tax, but that a preferential remission of it should be made in favour of the British Empire'. While Chamberlain was away, however, the free traders in the Cabinet, particularly C. T. Ritchie, who had succeeded Hicks Beach as Chancellor of the Exchequer in 1902, proposed not only to prevent the use of the corn duty for preferential tariffs but to repeal the duty itself. It was duly abolished in Ritchie's Budget, which infuriated Chamberlain and led to his launching a campaign on behalf of Tariff Reform in May.

The political repercussions were far-reaching and were to dominate British politics until the 1906 election. The Unionist party was deeply divided. Chamberlain's Tariff Reform League, inspired by Professor W. A. S. Hewins, helped to win over the local Unionist constituency parties to Tariff Reform, but not a single leading Unionist followed him. The free traders, moreover, included many prominent party figures, Devonshire, Goschen, Ritchie and St. Aldwyn (Hicks Beach); the latter founded the Free Food League to counter protectionist propaganda. Their disputes raged in and out of the Cabinet, taxing Balfour's powers of leadership to the utmost and finding them wanting. Balfour's attitude to Tariff Reform was dominated by his desire to preserve party unity and thus prevent a recurrence of the catastrophe that had befallen the party under Peel in 1846. As he could not convince himself of the merits of Tariff Reform on intellectual grounds, it is hardly surprising that he failed to convince the rest of his party. He thus adopted a defensive posture and compromised when the majority of his party looked to him for a firm lead. While a policy of 'trimming' could be justified purely on party grounds, it did not make for effective government, and there was a growing impression that Balfour was no longer in control of his Cabinet or his Party.

Balfour felt that Chamberlain had been badly treated in the decision to abolish the corn duty, but at the same time he did not want to lose leading members of his Cabinet. His own views were circulated in a Cabinet Memorandum entitled 'Notes on Insular Free Trade', where he argued that the Government should be able to threaten and use 'retaliations' in dealing with foreign governments. He went on to say that whereas imperial preference was very desirable to British trade and imperial unity, it was not yet a matter of practical politics. As a result, preference alone should be offered to the colonies, and the Government must avoid taxing food. Balfour's fine-spun arguments inevitably fell between two stools: the free traders were offended, while the tariff reformers felt that not enough would be done for the Empire, the initial reason for Chamberlain's campaign. The showdown in the Cabinet came in September 1903. A series of intrigues, misunderstandings, and accidents upset Balfour's attempts to find a modus vivendi. Confusion surrounds the circumstances in which the leading figures in the drama—Ritchie, Chamberlain and Devonshire—resigned, but it can be partly explained by Balfour's deliberate attempt to salvage as much party unity as he could. The Unionists were irrevocably split, even though Balfour tried to reconstruct his Cabinet to keep the balance between the opposing wings of the party: Austen Chamberlain, Joseph's son, was made Chancellor of the Exchequer, while Victor Cavendish, Devonshire's nephew and heir, became Financial Secretary to the Treasury. This appearance of unity deceived no one.

The Government's position in Parliament was increasingly difficult. Its majority could not be relied on for a vote on the fiscal question. In February 1904, 25 Unionists voted with the Opposition in a Parliamentary division, while the following month over 100 Protectionist 'whole-hoggers' rebelled against Balfour's policy of 'retaliation', which had become the official policy of the Unionist party. Faced with the prospect of defeat on several occasions in 1904-5, Balfour and his supporters resorted to the negative tactics of abstaining. Balfour could not bring himself to adopt the Tariff Reform programme, for he knew that food taxes would bring a terrible electoral defeat. He wrote as follows to Joseph Chamberlain on 18 February 1905: 'The prejudice against a small tax on food is not the fad of a few imperfectly informed theorists: it is a deep-rooted prejudice affecting a large mass of voters, especially the poorest class, which it will be a matter of extreme difficulty to overcome. I confess that it seemed to me last night that you underrated this difficulty.' But Chamberlain rejected Balfour's attempts to reconcile their differences, for by now the Tariff Reform issue had turned into a struggle for control of the Unionist party's organisation and determination of its policies for the future. The Chamberlainites, who represented the new Conservative industrial forces, were apparently out to democratise the party and direct it from below. By 1905 they had captured the constituency committees, the National Union, the Unionist press, and everything except the Central Office, which remained loyal to Balfour. 'What Balfour dreaded was precisely the tariff reformers' popular appeal, which, once sanctioned by the official leaders, would quickly transform the Unionist party into a democratic organisation run by protectionist squires and manufacturers.' His sympathies, therefore, were with the 'Free Fooders', who represented the old conservative landed classes and wanted the party to cling to its traditional base of established Church, landed interest, and House of Lords, with power wielded from above.

The general impression that Balfour and the Unionists had outstayed their time was confirmed by a flood of by-election reverses in 1904-5. Liberal Imperialists and Gladstonian Liberals welcomed this opportunity to sink their differences in the good old cause of free trade and to end the Unionist years of power. Tariff Reform, which had destroyed the unity of the Unionist party and alienated public opinion, was perhaps the most important single reason for the Liberals' success in 1906. It remained, however, to divide the Unionists and lose them future elections, prompting the interesting observation of Robert Blake: 'Seldom has a party persisted so long in such an unpromising cause. It almost gives credibility to the notion that there can be such a thing as a political death wish, improbable though that must seem amidst the normal wholesome pragmatism of British politicians.'

3 Taff Vale, 'Chinese Slavery', unemployment The disillusionment of the working classes with the Unionist party was far advanced by 1902. Social reforms had been promised and enough had been forthcoming between 1874 and 1895 to gain and to retain the electoral support of a large number of newly enfranchised working men, but subsequently, preoccupation with the Empire had deflected the Unionist party from domestic reform: the Boer War caused the postponement of Chamberlain's promise of old age pensions and no attempt had been made to satisfy demands for an eight-hour day. Working men were becoming impatient. Their patriotic feelings for the Empire, which the Unionists had exploited to win the 'Khaki' Election in 1900, were waning. Moreover, the Unionist ministry was to reveal that Balfour and his colleagues were lukewarm towards working-class demands. This failure of Conservative policy consolidated the working man's loss of confidence in the party and was responsible for driving him back to the Liberals or, alternatively, pushing him into the arms of the newly-founded Labour Representation Committee.

The Taff Vale Railway case in 1901 put to the test the Government's attitude towards industrial relations. The case originated in a dispute in South Wales, where railwaymen, aggrieved by the lack of union recognition and low wages, had gone on strike. The Taff Vale Railway Company sued the trade union concerned, the Amalgamated Society of Railway Servants, for loss of funds incurred through the strike. Two important principles were at stake. Could a trade union be sued and forced to pay damages for wrongs done by its members? And was it also exposed to the risk of an injunction (an inhibitory writ by which a superior court stops or prevents inequitable or illegal acts being done)? Hitherto the trade unions had assumed that their activities were covered and their funds protected by the Trade Union Acts of 1871 and 1875. In the High Court, however, Mr. Justice Farwell gave judgement in the plaintiff's favour. The railwaymen had the judgement reversed in the Court of Appeal, but then five law lords in the House of Lords, acting as the final court of appeal, upheld Farwell's judgement in favour of the Taff Vale Railway Company. The union had to pay £23,000 in costs and damages, in addition to its own legal costs. Judgement in an almost simultaneous trade union case, *Quinn v. Leathem*, emphasised the liability of union funds for damages. Future strike action would appear to have been drastically curtailed by these legal decisions. The trade union movement looked to the Government for redress, but Balfour's short-sightedness was reflected in his unwillingness either to reverse by legislation the more restrictive interpretation that was being placed by the courts on the trade union laws of 1871-5.

The unions were adamant that the Taff Vale verdict must be repealed as quickly as possible and were convinced that it was imperative to build up an independent political party in Parliament to help achieve this. The L.R.C. rapidly became the workers' main hope of reversing the Taff Vale decision, and the official membership of the party leapt from 376,000 in 1901 to 469,000 in 1902 and 861,000 in 1903. In February 1903, a parliamentary fund was set up for paying election expenses, and, at the rate of £200 a year, to enable successful candidates to accept the unsalaried office of M.P. Each affiliated society was to contribute annually into the fund a sum equivalent to a penny per member.

Through the creation of this considerable supply of money, the L.R.C. took an important step forward: not only did it widen the scope of independent political action, but it impressed interested observers at Liberal party headquarters.

There was a growing feeling that some understanding between the L.R.C. and the Liberals should be reached in order to prevent a split vote on the Left in elections, resulting in the return of a Unionist candidate on a minority vote. The L.R.C.'s sounder financial backing and a notable by-election success at Clitheroe in 1902 made a L.R.C.—Liberal rapprochement a matter of urgency for some Liberal party chiefs, despite the strong opposition of local Liberal leaders to any such arrangement. The Liberal Chief Whip, Herbert Gladstone, recognised the value of an understanding with Labour that would not split the vote on the Left and which would at the same time save party funds. He did not foresee that the emergence of the L.R.C. would produce a fundamental political upheaval, threatening the long-established parties. His decision in 1903 to support a Lib-Lab pact must be seen in the long term as an important moment in the fortunes of the Liberal and Labour parties; in the short term it was vital in the Liberals' triumph in 1906.

Ramsay MacDonald was equally opportunist, being prepared to compromise socialist principles and to deceive his colleagues in order to get the L.R.C. into Parliament and keep it there. He offered to start informal talks, and Gladstone sent Jesse Herbert to investigate further. MacDonald provided a list of constituencies where an electoral arrangement between the Liberals and the L.R.C. would be desirable. Secret discussions continued, and, by March, Gladstone was prepared to use his financial control over the local Liberal associations in certain working-class constituencies in order to request them 'to abstain from nominating a Liberal candidate and to unite in support of any recognised and competent Labour candidate who [supported] the general objects of the Liberal party'. A campaign to educate the local party organisations to accept the policy of Liberal headquarters was under way by May 1903, and Chamberlain's decision to launch his campaign for Tariff Reform that same month made a

Lib-Lab understanding easier. Philip Snowden, one of the L.R.C. leaders, published a pamphlet entitled 'The Chamberlain Bubble' late in 1903 which attacked Tariff Reform and sold nearly 40,000 copies. A sensational by-election victory by an L.R.C. candidate, Arthur Henderson, over Unionist and Liberal opponents made Gladstone even more prepared to settle with MacDonald. Accordingly Gladstone sent Campbell-Bannerman, his party leader, a list of 35 seats in which L.R.C. candidates were confirmed or likely to be chosen, and where he could see no objection to giving them a free hand. The secret Lib-Lab pact that was finally concluded was in no way a formal alliance: it was to apply for one election, a bargain which assured the Liberal party of victory in the coming election at the expense of a greatly increased Labour representation in Parliament.

Labour's chances showed no marked advance by 1905. The group of L.R.C. M.P.s did not make a conspicuous impact in the Commons; they were too few to be effective, and their attempts to secure changes in the trade union laws in 1903, 1904 and 1905 were in vain. The party was more successful in the constituencies, with the result that, by 1906, there were seventy-six local L.R.C. parties in addition to affiliated trade councils. In 1904 the contributions by party members to the L.R.C. parliamentary fund were made compulsory and further strengthened the party's finances. MacDonald and Hardie continued to shape a Labour policy for the coming election which could attract Liberal trade unionists as well as retaining the support of committed socialists. Unpopular Government policies in 1904-5 once again stimulated working-class discontent, and provided the Opposition parties with a platform which they did not hesitate to exploit.

The 'Chinese Labour' question was one such issue. Milner, the British High Commissioner in South Africa, had been anxious for a speedy reconstruction after the Boer War. To meet a shortage of native labour in the Rand mines, the mineowners, wishing to make greater profits, pressed Milner for permission to import Chinese coolies as cheap labour. Alfred Lyttleton, the Colonial Secretary, did not have the political standing to resist

Milner, and Balfour's approval was obtained. Twenty thousand Chinese labourers had been imported by 1904, and 47,000 by the following year. The issue of 'Chinese Slavery' aroused a great outcry. It was a perfect example of Balfour's failure to appeal to the middle ground in politics and of his insensitivity towards the working class. His Government seemed to be reasserting a commodity view of labour. If Colonial capitalists were allowed the right to meet an industrial labour shortage by importing 'foreigners', the precedent might be applied in Britain and working-class aspirations for greater industrial freedom undermined. Furthermore, for racial reasons, the coolies were not imported as freemen, but as indentured labour, which ensured that they would work long enough to cover the costs of recruitment and transport. They had to live segregated in compounds, which they were forbidden to leave for more than forty-eight hours at a time. They could neither settle nor buy land in South Africa, and were subject to a particularly harsh penal code. By the end of 1904, only two out of 27,000 Chinese labourers had their wives with them; the 'humanitarian conscience' of many members of the middle class was outraged by accounts of 'slavery', while Nonconformists protested at the 'nameless practices' (sexual irregularities) reported from the compounds. The political scandal that ensued had not abated by 1906, and it certainly harmed the Unionists at the polls.

The Government's apparent indifference towards the less fortunate members of society was again illustrated by its failure to relieve the high level of unemployment in the years 1904-5. The Unionist party still believed in the Victorian approach to unemployment, as embodied in the Poor Law of 1834, which was now out of date. On ideological grounds they were opposed to any solution that would smack of collectivism. Walter Long, the President of the Local Government Board, was sympathetic, however, and in November 1904, proposed a scheme to deal with the unemployment problem in London. Joint committees of guardians, local councillors, and members of charity organisations were set up in each London borough to provide money, information and casual employment for the temporarily unemployed, and to refer the permanently unemployed to the work-house. The scheme had to be financed by charity; Long was opposed to Treasury aid, and hardly any ratepayers' money was provided. Although some 46,000 applications for help were received by the committees, of which 26,000 were recognised as eligible, it is doubtful whether more than 5000 obtained permanent work. The scheme was obviously inadequate, and there were 'hunger marches' and demonstrations by the unemployed. The Government, conscious of the failure of its 1904-5 experiment, was forced to take more positive action. The Unemployed Workmen Bill (1905) was the result. The Bill made it possible for the 1904 scheme to be extended to most authorities. They were given powers to add to the voluntary resources available for unemployment relief the product of a local rate of not more than a penny in the pound. 'Distress committees' were to keep labour registers, to investigate need and provide work. A special charitable fund, the Queen's Fund, amounting to £153,000, raised in response to a public appeal by Queen Alexandra, provided the major financial resources for the committees.

Mr. Maurice Bruce has called the Bill 'a new departure, a tacit admission of state responsibility, which, however limited its intention and effect, could never be reversed'. This may explain why it was strongly resisted and chopped about in committee by diehard Unionists, and why it was carried only with Opposition support. Moreover, the regulations issued by the Local Government Board in October 1905 limited the scope of the scheme still further; destitution rather than unemployment seemed to be the qualification. It was not surprising, therefore, that the Bill failed to solve the problem of unemployment; the help it provided was only temporary and it did not attack the roots of the problem. The Government's failure to provide adequate remedies for the unemployment problem helped to widen the breach which now existed between the Unionist party and the labouring classes.

4 The defeat of the Unionists 1905-6   The collapse of Balfour's Ministry had been hourly expected. The Government's widespread unpopularity and internal feuds had rendered its electoral prospects hopeless. A depressing run of by-election defeats began at Norwich in January 1904. Two Unionists had been returned unopposed here in 1900, but on this occasion, the Unionist, a moderate tariff reformer, was opposed by Labour and Liberal candidates, and the Liberal was elected with a majority of almost 2000. Balfour himself considered that defeat was imminent. He had lost his appetite for politics, but clung to office in order to have sufficient time to renovate the Imperial Defence Committee and to cement the Entente Cordiale before the probable return to power of the Liberals. His Ministry had ended Britain's dangerous isolation by the conclusion of the Anglo-Japanese Alliance (1902) and the Anglo-French Entente (1904). The First Sea Lord, Sir John Fisher, had started to introduce those changes that were soon to revolutionise the British Navy, and Balfour had himself put the Committee of Imperial Defence on an effective footing. Such measures were a tribute to Balfour's vision and statesmanship, but they did not win his party any votes. He was, alas, a poor Prime Minister, who could neither hold his Cabinet and party together nor lead a nation-wide campaign to win back public support. Under his inert leadership it was almost inevitable that the Unionist Party should slide to defeat.

Balfour's last desperate gamble was to exploit the rifts among his Liberal opponents. Although the Liberal factions had re-united over free trade, serious differences of opinion on defence, foreign policy and Home Rule continued to bedevil relations between the Gladstonian Liberals, led by Campbell-Bannerman, and the Liberal Imperialists, who looked to Rosebery for inspiration. Balfour felt confident that a general election in 1906 following a period of Liberal rule would be more likely to benefit the Unionists than an election in 1905, when the electorate was evidently reacting against a long period of Unionist government. By resigning rather than dissolving Parliament, he wanted to involve the Liberals in the difficult business of forming a government and producing a coherent policy before going to the nation. He was hopeful that Campbell-Bannerman would not be able to appoint a ministry, or, if he did succeed, that his party would soon split. So, on 4 December 1905, Balfour resigned, and the next day Campbell-Bannerman took office. Asa Briggs has described this moment as 'the great turning point in Edwardian politics, although it was not clearly recognised at the time . . . Balfour's would-be adroit tactical resignation was the prelude to a major shift in democratic politics. The Unionists did not regain power until the 1920s.'

Not until King Edward sent for Campbell-Bannerman had it been certain that he would be the new Prime Minister. It was agreed that Asquith should be Chancellor of the Exchequer and Leader of the House of Commons, Grey Foreign Secretary, and Haldane Secretary for War; Rosebery was given no appointment. Campbell-Bannerman completed a strong administration by appointing Lloyd George to the Board of Trade, John Burns, the former labour leader, to the Local Government Board, and Winston Churchill, the dynamic young member for Oldham who had left the Unionist party over Tariff Reform in 1904, to the Under-Secretaryship for the Colonies. The need for Liberal unity on the eve of an election had dominated Campbell-Bannerman's thoughts. The new Premier enhanced his reputation during the transfer of power; he had, in November, reconciled his followers to a 'step by step' policy on Home Rule, and now, with a united party and a brilliant team behind him, he approached the forthcoming election with confidence. Balfour's gamble had misfired. When Parliament was dissolved on 8 January, one of the most exciting and significant elections for many years began.

The General Election of 1906 was contested on a great variety of issues, some national, some local, while certain candidates added a flavour of their own to the campaign. In some areas it was 'Chinese Slavery', elsewhere 'class war', or again 'Home Rule' that made the headlines. But there seems little doubt, that the major issue was 'Tariff Reform versus Free Trade'. Campbell-Bannerman had begun the campaign with a major speech in which he outlined a moderate programme designed to win the vital middle ground. He defended free trade, made some guarded comments on Home Rule, and pledged continuity in foreign policy. He promised changes in trade union legislation, a ban on the further import of Chinese coolies into South Africa, and social reform. The L.R.C., mindful as ever of the need to steer a middle way between Liberalism and Socialism, made little reference to the latter in its election manifesto and concentrated on wooing the trade union vote. The Unionists, exhausted after ten years in office, bankrupt of ideas, and divided on the vital matter of Tariff Reform, were forced on the defensive. They had no way of appeasing the general hostility they had aroused during their years in power.

There were no professional pollsters and no public opinion surveys to forecast the result when polling began on 12 January 1906. A Unionist defeat was expected, but many unknown factors, such as the number of uncontested seats in 1900, made accurate predictions hazardous. The results were astonishing. The Liberal party won a landslide victory. Four hundred and one Liberals were elected, including 24 Lib-Labs, mostly miners; there were also 29 L.R.C. candidates and 83 Irish Nationalists returned. Unionist representation fell dramatically from 402 to 157, of whom 11 were Unionist Free Traders, 36 'Balfourites', and the rest 'Chamberlainites'. Balfour himself was defeated in Manchester. His biographer has written that 'this election which ended almost twenty years of Conservative domination, was the greatest cataclysm in the Party's history'. It was an electoral revolution, producing the largest majority for any government since 1832.

As research into the history of elections is still incomplete, one cannot be certain what caused this great swing away from the Unionists. The Unionist vote per opposed candidate (c 4300) was about the same as in 1900, but the Liberal vote rose by over twenty-five per cent (from c 4100 to c 5200). These figures suggest that there was no mass conversion to Liberalism, but rather that many who had abstained in 1900 were sufficiently antagonistic to subsequent Unionist policies to support the anti-government vote in 1906. The Lib-Lab pact made the Government's rout the more complete in terms of seats. The pact had benefited both sides, ensuring a Liberal government with a large majority and Labour's emergence as a Third Party. One could argue that the Liberals sowed the seeds of their own destruction in allowing Labour to capture so many seats, but to the Liberal leaders at the time the results were 'astoundingly good'. As Jesse Herbert wrote to Gladstone, 'the sum of the matter is that in England and Wales, Liberals and Labour hold 367 seats, i.e. a majority of 239, and there are only two cases in which we have just grounds for complaint against the Labour people, and one case where they have just grounds for complaint against us. Was there ever such a justification of policy by results?' Just as more efficient party organisation had helped to win the election for the Liberals and Labour, so the decay and dissension in the Unionist party were an important factor in its fall. The Chief Whip since 1902, Acland Hood, was insufficiently forceful, and his efforts were hampered by the bitter struggle for control of the party's organisation that had begun in 1903. The Unionist party seemed to have forgotten who the real enemy was.

A more detailed study of those areas which the Unionists lost in 1906 would appear to reveal some specific reasons for their failure. The loss of working-class constituencies in Lancashire and London which they had held in 1900 would seem to confirm that a significant number of working-class votes had turned against them: they were now paying the price for their neglect of social reform, Taff Vale, 'Chinese Slavery', and 'the big loaf and the little loaf'. Moreover, a fifteen per cent swing against the party in the well-to-do London seats would suggest that ground had been lost with middle-class voters: Nonconformist, temperance, and humanitarian interests were hostile to the Unionists' handling of education, the licensing laws, and Chinese labour. Blake has put forward the interesting and convincing hypothesis that 'a rebellion by the intellectuals usually accompanies and probably in some measure causes a great political shift, a major loss of central ground, such as evidently occurred at this time'. He suggests that with the Home Rule issue, never a happy stamping-ground for intellectuals, temporarily in abeyance, and with their disenchantment towards the 'imperial idea' after the Boer War, they were ready to listen to the Liberals, who seemed to have recovered their unity and their sense of purpose and were ploughing the middle ground so effectively. The Liberals won the 1906 election because of the way in which they capitalised the Unionists' mistakes and unpopularity. Their promise to repeal the 1902 Education Act and their hostility to the 1904 Licensing Act, which they castigated as a 'brewers' Bill' because it established the principle of compensation for redundant public-houses, had reforged the old alliance with the Nonconformists and the temperance reformers that had worked so well in the past. Their opposition to 'food taxes', 'Chinese Slavery', Taff Vale, and unemployment, and the hope that they would bring social reform, had helped to convert many working-class voters. The talented ministerial team that Campbell-Bannerman had assembled and the 'new look' liberalism that was emerging seemed to the electorate a far better prospect than the exhausted and socially divisive ideals of the Unionist party.

Balfour's own explanation of his defeat is interesting. Writing privately to Lady Salisbury soon after the election he had this to say: 'What has occurred has nothing whatever to do with any of the things we have been squabbling over the last few years. Campbell-Bannerman is a mere cork, dancing in a torrent which he cannot control, and what is going on here is a faint echo of the same movement which has produced massacres in St. Petersburg, riots in Vienna, and socialist processions in Berlin.' Later he wrote to Austen Chamberlain forecasting that the outcome would be the break-up of the Liberal party. Balfour was devastatingly correct in his analysis of the Liberals' future, but seriously mistaken in predicting a Socialist-inspired revolution in Britain. The next few years were indeed violent, but this was primarily the result of the hysterical policies pursued by a Unionist Opposition which Balfour himself led until 1911, when he was pushed out and replaced by Bonar Law as party leader.

Chapter III

The Liberals and the Lords 1906-11

1 Rejection of measures 1906-8 The Liberal triumph in 1906 ushered in a long period of Liberal rule. At the same time, it led to one of the most bitter disputes in recent constitutional history, and to a crisis which threatened the delicate relationship between the Monarchy, the House of Commons, and the House of Lords. The Unionist party must to a large extent be held responsible for what happened since it was determined to retain its monopoly of power, in spite of its decisive defeat at the polls. Balfour was expressing a commonly felt Unionist view when he told a public meeting at Nottingham in 1906, 'The great Unionist party should still control, whether in power or opposition, the destinies of this great Empire.' The years between 1906 and 1914 were to see the Unionist party attempting to prove that this was no empty threat.

The 1906 election had revealed a distinct swing in public opinion towards the parties of the Left. It seemed that democracy had at last arrived, and that a radical restructuring of long-established institutions would inevitably follow. The Unionist party, however, set out to frustrate the wishes of the people by a vigorous defence of existing policies and institutions. Its enormous majority in the House of Lords was the last remaining stronghold of Unionism, and it was the indiscriminate use of this power which ultimately led to the Parliament Act of 1911 restricting the Lords' veto.

The composition of the House of Commons was transformed by the election. Two hundred and twenty of the 401 Liberals were new members, as were most of the 29 Labour M.P.s. The old pre-eminence of the landed classes had been successfully challenged by the business and professional classes. All the Labour members were of working-class origin. Many M.P.s were people of modest means. It was to such men that the destinies of Great Britain and her Empire had been committed, and yet to Balfour and Lord Lansdowne, the Unionist leaders, it was out of the question that men of such lowly background should wrest the mantle of leadership from them. Like Lord Salisbury before them, they were aristocrats who believed that it was the aristocracy which had made Britain great, and that the parliamentary system had functioned so successfully in the nineteenth century only because the upper classes had continued to govern. Tory democracy as defined by Disraeli had been based on the assumption that the larger the electorate, the stronger would be the position of the old ruling classes as against middle-class upstarts, and in practice the aristocracy continued to dominate both Unionist and Liberal Governments up to 1905. The new House of Commons appeared to pose a further threat to the old order. Under Balfour and Lansdowne, aristocratic England was determined to resist this renewed challenge to its traditional leadership.

Of the 602 peers, only 83 described themselves as Liberals; 355 were Conservative Unionists and 124 were Liberal Unionists. This Unionist predominance in the Upper House can be traced back to the numerous creations of peers in the late eighteenth century. These Conservative forces had increased in number during the nineteenth century, but only occasionally had a Conservative House of Lords clashed with a Whig or Liberal majority in the House of Commons. In 1832, for example, the Conservative peers had passed the Reform Bill only after the threat of a royal creation of Whig peers. But in general the Upper House had adopted a cautious and non-partisan attitude, rejecting those measures, such as Gladstone's Paper Duties, with which it disagreed without unduly provoking the elected government of the day. However, during the long Conservative ascendancy between 1874 and 1905 the Lords were more openly partisan, uttering hardly a murmur against any Conservative measure but contemptuously destroying Gladstone's Second Irish Home Rule Bill in 1893. Their lordships were acutely aware that their political leadership and their wealth were once again, as in 1832 and in 1846, gravely threatened by the new democratic forces, and they were prepared to defend their traditional powers regardless of the political consequences.

It can be argued, however, as a defence of the actions of the Unionist peers in the pre-war years that they were reacting against the forces of change in a characteristic way. They were conservatives by birth and upbringing and were thus naturally opposed to those changes which undermined their way of life. After the Unionist débâcle in the 1906 election, they alone had the power to uphold vital Unionist interests against the attacks of their Liberal and Socialist adversaries. As Sir Philip Magnus has pointed out, 'No Englishman of any class would have hesitated before 1914 to exact the maximum advantage from any customary or legal privilege which he possessed; and the Peers, who had merely registered approval of Conservative measures for many years, would have been ashamed not to assert their full rights against the Liberal Government in 1906.' In fact, the Unionist peers looked forward confidently to the coming battle, and were particularly amenable to the political manoeuvres devised by the party leadership for the new Parliament.

Balfour's tactics of using the Unionist peers to destroy the Liberals' legislative programme were an attempt to meet the demands of his party for more forthright leadership and more militant policies. The Tariff Reformers blamed him for failing to convert the British electorate to their new protectionist policies, and they were justified in their criticism, since Balfour's 'trimming' policy on Tariff Reform had not helped the party in its last years in office. The Tariff Reformers did not, however, doubt the validity of their case in 1906, nor did they accept the fact that it had been their programme which had largely contributed to the Unionists' rout at the election. However, in spite of causing the Unionist defeat, 109 of the 157 Unionist M.P.s in the new House of Commons were Tariff Reformers. Thus

Tariff Reform had to remain in the forefront of the Party's policies, even though Balfour might have preferred to drop it. Indeed, Joseph Chamberlain might have replaced Balfour as party leader had he not been struck down with paralysis in July 1906. Balfour remained as party leader in spite of the widespread dissatisfaction of Unionists with his uninspiring leadership. His unscrupulous use of the Unionist majority in the Lords was one way of appeasing his critics.

Kenneth Young, Balfour's most recent biographer, has gallantly defended Balfour's conduct in these years. While frankly admitting his deficiencies as a leader of men, Young praises Balfour's mastery of political tactics and claims that he must not be held responsible for causing the dangerous constitutional situation that arose. He would have us believe that Balfour was as much a victim of the prevailing political hysteria as were his Liberal opponents. It is nevertheless difficult to escape from the conclusion that the Unionist leader must himself take much of the blame for the bitterness and constitutional tumult which his policies provoked. By 1906 his detachment from democracy was complete, and his obstructionist attitude was finely calculated. He saw no purpose in giving his party a constructive policy whilst in opposition; he believed that the real business of an opposition was to oppose. He found willing accomplices in the Conservative peers.

The political battle commenced when, on 9 April 1906, the Government brought in an Education Bill designed to remedy Nonconformist grievances against the 1902 Act. The Bill, moreover, could be considered to reflect the wishes of the electorate, since the Nonconformist vote had made an important contribution to the Liberals' victory. Not surprisingly the Bill gave rise to a storm of protest from Unionists and Anglicans, and they decided to reject it. Balfour's tactics were swiftly revealed when the peers allowed the Bill through on its second reading and then so changed it in Committee that its original purpose was reversed: the amended Bill would have given the advocates of denominational teaching an even more advantageous position than they already enjoyed under the 1902 Act. The Commons totally rejected the

Lords' amendments, and when conciliatory Government proposals were refused by Balfour, the Government had no alternative but to abandon the Bill in December 1906. The important
Plural Voting Bill, which would have restricted to one vote those
electors who previously had several, was also mauled by the Lords
and withdrawn by the Government.

The strictly partisan nature of Unionist policy can again be
seen in regard to the third controversial Government measure
of the 1906 session, the Trade Disputes Bill. A Royal Commission
set up in 1903 had reported in favour of radically altering the
effect of the legal decisions in the Taff Vale and *Quinn v. Leathem*
cases on industrial relations. The Government, while accepting
the principle that trade union funds should be given greater
protection, was deeply divided as to how this should be done.
Moreover, when the Government's Bill was introduced, it
received an unfriendly reception from both Labour M.P.s and
the trade union movement. A Labour member, Hudson,
brought forward a Private Member's Bill based on an alternative
approach to the problem. In the course of the debates on the
Government's Bill, the Prime Minister, Campbell-Bannerman,
changed his mind and incorporated Hudson's Bill into the Government measure. This last-minute change satisfied the Commons
and the Bill was passed. Here was legislation which the Lords
might have been expected to reject, for not only was it damaging
to Unionist interests, but it was a hastily conceived measure on
which the Lords could properly exercise its constitutional
function of checking and amending. Their lordships, however,
thought only in terms of party tactics, not constitutional duty.
They did not want to provoke the Labour movement at this
stage, and preferred to play on the dissensions which the Bill
had earlier caused between Campbell-Bannerman and Asquith.
The Trades Disputes Bill was therefore allowed to become law
with little argument. The Lords then continued to wreck the
Government's major legislative proposals in the 1907 parliamentary session. Four Land Bills, which would have met long-
standing Liberal and Labour desires for land reform, were
either rejected or so mutilated as to be of little value.

While the Unionists rejoiced at the Government's legislative impotence in its first two years of office, Liberal tempers became frayed. Churchill referred to the Lords in February 1907 as 'the fortress of negation and reaction', and Lloyd George in a memorable attack stated that 'the House of Lords has long ceased to be the watchdog of the constitution. It has become Mr. Balfour's poodle. It barks for him. It fetches and carries for him. It bites anybody he sets it on to.' The Liberals were in a serious dilemma. While they were aware that the measures which the Lords had rejected had been electorally popular, they also knew full well that they could afford neither the expense nor the risk of fighting a General Election so shortly after the last one. The party's leaders, denied the advantages of public opinion polls, were nevertheless conscious that public opinion had been abnormally volatile in the 1906 election and that the Unionists would recapture some of their lost strongholds as the electorate returned to its traditional behaviour. Some Liberals argued that a policy of 'Filling the Cup' should be pursued, whereby the Lords would be openly invited to reject so many measures that they would demonstrate their foolishness, and at the same time offend all those interests from which the Liberal party drew its support. An alternative view was that the Government should water down controversial measures and frame only compromise legislation which had some hope of passing the Lords. Campbell-Bannerman, having listened to these opinions and to the suggestions of a Cabinet Committee on Lords reform set up in 1907, decided to revive in a Memorandum John Bright's old scheme of a suspensory veto, restricting the Lords' right of delay to two sessions, after which the measure would become law. This Memorandum was then turned into a Resolution which was presented to the Commons on 24 June 1907, when, after a three-day debate, it was passed by 432 votes to 147. However, apart from rallying Liberal morale, the Resolution had no immediate effect on the powers of the peers. Campbell-Bannerman was not yet prepared to take immediate constitutional action against the Lords, and, when he resigned through ill-health in April 1908, neither was his successor Asquith.

The 1908 session followed the pattern set in 1906 and 1907. The Government's only notable legislative success was the Old Age Pensions Bill (*see* p. 81). The Lords had intended to amend this measure but had refrained when the Commons had said that a question of 'privilege' was at stake. They had no such scruples about attacking the Licensing Bill, another controversial measure. Here was a well-framed Bill, warmly supported by the temperance movement and by religious organisations, which sought to lessen the evils of intemperance by reducing the number of public houses so that they should not in any area exceed a fixed ratio to the population. The Unionists, however, chose to support the brewing interest, which contributed so handsomely to party funds, and the Bill was killed on its second reading in the Lords. Thus, as Roy Jenkins has aptly remarked, 'The Liberal Government looked increasingly becalmed in the lee of the House of Lords.' The failure of the Government to live up to expectation was reflected in a series of by-election reverses in 1908. That same year saw a depression in trade and rising unemployment. The Unionists were jubilant at the success of their obstructionist policies and confidently predicted victory in the next election. A dissolution of Parliament at this time was from the Government's point of view out of the question, and yet it had somehow to restore its authority if it was to retain and rally its supporters. This was the situation which gave rise to the People's Budget.

2 The People's Budget 1909-10   Lloyd George had succeeded Asquith as Chancellor of the Exchequer in 1908, and it was his 'People's Budget' on 29 April 1909 which was the Government's answer to both its critics and its followers. It precipitated the constitutional crisis which ended two years later in the Parliament Act, which curtailed the Lords' veto. How far it was deliberately framed to provoke a clash with the Lords remains a matter of some controversy. Malcolm Thomson, the official biographer of Lloyd George, claims that Lloyd George with Asquith's approval intentionally drafted his Budget so as to court its rejection by the peers. This would appear to be in accordance with the Chancellor's increasing resentment at the irresponsible conduct of the

Lords and with his strong desire to reduce their powers. However, Roy Jenkins, author of *Mr. Balfour's Poodle*, puts forward the interesting opinion that it never seriously occurred to the Government that the Lords would dare to challenge the Commons' supremacy in financial matters by attacking a Finance Bill. He argues that a controversial Budget was the Liberals' alternative to limiting the power of the House of Lords. The clash with the Upper House, rather than being planned, grew out of the course of events. Once the peers had been unwise enough to reject the Budget, the Liberals took the favourable opportunity of fighting them.

Lloyd George considered many other factors when drawing up his Budget. In the Cabinet discussions McKenna, the new First Lord of the Admiralty, proposed meeting Germany's challenge to Britain's traditional naval supremacy by asking that the 1909 estimates should provide for the building of six Dreadnoughts. This was opposed by the social reformers in the Cabinet, Churchill and Lloyd George, who maintained that four would be sufficient. Suspicions of Germany's intentions led to a vociferous public agitation, skilfully directed by the Unionists, which proclaimed, 'We want Eight, and we won't wait.' So the Cabinet decided to lay down eight Dreadnoughts at once. An additional item of expenditure would be the new pensions scheme, in operation for a full year for the first time, and expected to cost an extra six million pounds. The Treasury had estimated a deficit of some sixteen million pounds for 1909-10. Lloyd George would have to find new sources of revenue to meet the pressing needs of national defence and social welfare. He could either impose tariffs, which would have pleased the Unionists but would have been incompatible with the Liberals' support for Free Trade, or increase taxation 'to make the poor richer and the rich poorer'. Lloyd George had to keep political considerations firmly before him. He must not only overcome objections from the Radicals to the increase in naval expenditure but also produce a reforming Budget in order to revive flagging Government morale. The success of the Old Age Pensions Bill had shown the Government that the only way of regaining legislative initiative from the Lords and of achieving its reforms was by incorporating controversial social or political proposals in money bills. The 1909 Finance Bill was an obvious opportunity for the Government to test their diagnosis of the situation.

Lloyd George's Budget speech was unimpressive, but it had the desired effect. Government supporters were cheered by his assertion that 'this is a War Budget. It is for raising money to wage implacable warfare against poverty and squalidness', while Balfour denounced it as 'vindictive, inequitable, based on no principle, and injurious to the productive capacity of the country'. In fact Lloyd George had largely relied on traditional sources of revenue. Tobacco, spirits, liquor licences and stamp duties were to yield an additional £6,750,000; income tax (up from 1/- to 1/2 in the £) and death duties were increased to produce an extra £5,500,000; £3,000,000 was deducted from the Sinking Fund.

Unionist fury, however, was concentrated on two proposals: the introduction of supertax at a rate of sixpence in the pound on the amount by which all incomes of £5000 or over exceeded £3000, and the Land Value Duties. A duty of twenty per cent on the unearned increase of land value was to be paid whenever land changed hands; a tax of a halfpenny in the pound was to be paid on the capital value of undeveloped land and minerals; and a ten per cent reversion duty was to be paid on any benefit which came to a lessor at the end of a lease. The Treasury expected these Land Value Duties to bring in £500,000 during the financial year 1909-10. Although Lloyd George may have seen the land taxes as a potentially lucrative source of income, they appear also to have served the immediate political purpose of provoking a conflict with the landed classes in which he could portray them as rich men trying to evade bearing their fair share of the nation's burdens. His calculation proved accurate, for it was around the land taxes and the land valuation clauses, skilfully inserted into the Finance Bill to facilitate the levy of this new form of taxation, that the opposition to the Budget crystallised. The landed classes interpreted the land taxes as a death-blow to their traditional power and this was why they determined to fight the Budget.

Lloyd George's proposals unleashed not only a bitter political struggle in Parliament, but also a nation-wide debate. A Budget Protest League, financed by bankers like the Rothschilds and publicised by the Harmsworth Press, was set up to discredit the Budget, while Churchill became President of a Budget League founded to extol its virtues. The political atmosphere in the summer of 1909 was remarkable for its hatreds, emotions, eloquence and continuing excitement. The landed classes, with the Dukes at their head, took up uncompromising positions in their protest against what Lord Lansdowne called 'a monument of reckless and improvident finance'. Their hatred was aimed at Lloyd George and Churchill in particular, and the Duke of Beaufort was echoing the sentiments of his class when he said that he would 'like to see Winston Churchill and Lloyd George in the middle of twenty couple of dog hounds'. Meanwhile, Lloyd George and Churchill, in a series of great speeches, increased the exasperation and truculence of their opponents by injecting the maximum amount of heat into an already tense situation. At Leicester on 4 September Churchill ridiculed Balfour, 'who aims to lead—who has been meaning to lead for six years if only he could find out where on earth to lead to'. He had this to say of the Lords: 'Do not let us be too hard on them. It is poor sport—almost like teasing goldfish. These ornamental creatures blunder on every hook they seek, and there is no sport whatever in trying to catch them.' This popular oratory reached its height in the speeches of Lloyd George at Newcastle-upon-Tyne in October. He warned the Lords, 'Let them realise what they are doing. They are forcing a Revolution. The Peers may decree a Revolution, but the people will direct it.' Lloyd George had by now recaptured popular approval for the Government and had provoked his opponents to their next false move—the Lords' rejection of the Budget.

By September 1909 public attention had shifted from the merits of the Budget to the wider constitutional issue that would be raised if the Lords rejected it. Asquith had by now become the main exponent of the Government's case, and he could not believe that the Lords would be so foolish as to contest the Commons' power of the purse, something they had not done for 250 years, yet still hope to retain popular approval for their action. Balfour, however, was assailed from all sections of the Unionist party with demands to reject the Finance Bill. Seriously miscalculating the degree of passion the Budget had aroused in the country, he once again decided to pander to the extremists in his party. If he had counselled patience and restraint, the Unionists could have capitalised on the pronounced swing in public opinion towards the Right: on the evidence of by-elections it was calculated in January 1909 that the Unionists would have won a majority of 100 in the event of a general election. Balfour preferred to use his powers in the Lords to reject a measure to which his party was opposed, even though it was contrary to established constitutional precedent. In September he made public his support for rejection. Thus Balfour's weak and misguided leadership escalated the clash over the Budget into a wider constitutional crisis between the Commons and the Lords—a crisis into which the Monarchy would inevitably be drawn.

Edward VII had viewed the sequence of events since the Liberals had taken office with increasing dismay, and he had therefore sought to allay the party strife by promoting policies of compromise and goodwill. However, he was uneasy at the radicalism of some members of his government, and relations between the King and his Ministers had noticeably deteriorated since the death of Campbell-Bannerman. The King continually complained to Asquith during the Budget agitation about the attacks made by Liberal ministers on the hereditary principle and about the violent language they employed. At the same time he was aware of the suicidal folly of the Lords should they decide to reject the Budget. Early in October the King urged the Unionist leaders to reach a compromise with the Government, but to no avail. In spite of this initial rebuff, it was the Crown which ultimately played the decisive part in resolving the constitutional crisis.

On 4 November 1909, after 554 divisions and a full 70 parliamentary days spent discussing it, the Finance Bill passed the

Commons. On 23 November the Budget debate began in the Lords, and after five days of bitter discussion, it was rejected on its second reading by 350 votes to 75. Asquith immediately dissolved Parliament on the ground that the Lords, by rejecting the Finance Bill, had acted unconstitutionally. Polling would begin on 15 January 1910, and would last a fortnight. The election campaign was notable for the high quality of the speeches, and for the active participation of the peers in the election, contrary to the parliamentary precedent that no member of the Lords should concern himself in elections to the House of Commons. Public interest ran high, and although the question of the Lords' veto was of major importance, the outcome of the election was determined on the more understandable issue of the merits of the Budget as opposed to Tariff Reform.

The election result showed that British politics had reverted to their normal pattern after the extraordinary result in 1906. The Liberals had won 275 seats, the Unionists 273, Labour 40, and the Irish Nationalists 82: the Unionists had regained most of the English county seats they had lost in 1906 as well as a number of small urban constituencies. Although the result was disappointing for the Government, it was a serious reversal for the Unionists, who had confidently expected victory. Asquith could, moreover, with the support of his Labour and Irish allies, still count on an overall majority of 124 over the Unionists.

The Liberal Government achieved little between January and April 1910, and it has been argued that this was due to their reliance on Irish and Labour votes. The Irish were hostile towards the Budget, since it had offended the distillers and publicans on whose contributions they were dependent. It appears, however, that this factor has been exaggerated, since the Government was seeking the reform of the Lords, which Labour and Irish members could not fail to support since it would clear the way for the reforms they wanted. Moreover, the Liberals, after their successful solution of the South African question, were now more prepared to grant Home Rule to Ireland, 'to make Redmond the Irish Botha', and the Nationalist M.P.s could not fail to support them.

Asquith did not press home his numerical advantage in the new Parliament. He was unwilling to force the issue with the Lords, and he had not obtained from King Edward 'guarantees' that sufficient new peers would be created to break the resistance of the Upper House if it were necessary. The latter omission was particularly unfortunate since Asquith had given the impression in a speech on 10 December 1909, before the dissolution of Parliament, that he had obtained such 'guarantees'. In fact, on 15 December the King had refused to give them until after a second general election. Asquith could see that without them the problem of the House of Lords was almost insoluble. On 21 February 1910 he told the Commons that he had obtained no 'guarantees', nor had he asked for them. Confronted with Cabinet divisions over the extent of Lords reform, Irish refusal to vote for the Budget unless a veto bill was first passed and Unionist charges that he was buying office at the expense of corrupt concessions to Redmond, Asquith fell back on his policy of 'Wait and See', and did nothing.

On 21 March Asquith began an attack on the powers of the Upper House, thus bringing the quarrel between the Commons and the Lords to its final and decisive stage. The Commons debated Three Resolutions containing the Government's proposals on Lords reform. The Lords could neither amend nor reject a money bill, defined as such by the Speaker of the House of Commons, and could only delay other legislation up to two years and one month. A Bill passed by the Commons would become law without the assent of the peers if, on the third occasion, it had not been passed by the Lords without amendments other than those agreed to by both Houses, within twenty-eight days of being received by the Upper House. The maximum duration of Parliament was to be reduced from seven to five years. The Commons passed the Resolutions on 14 April, and on that same day they were incorporated into the Parliament Bill, which was introduced and read for the first time. Reform of the composition of the Lords would be a task for the future; the Bill concentrated on the more urgent objective of restricting the existing powers of the Upper House. Asquith's handling of the Resolutions was skilful, and he proceeded to tell the Commons categorically that he would obtain the 'guarantees' from the King. By ruthless use of the closure the Budget was pushed through the Commons by 27 April, and the Lords let it through without a division on the following day. It received the Royal Assent on 29 April, and Parliament was adjourned.

It was during this short recess that the sudden death of King Edward occurred on 6 May. It was clear that the impending conflict with the Lords would have to be temporarily postponed because of the new King's political inexperience.

3 The Parliament Bill 1910-11   George V was, in the words of his biographer, Sir Harold Nicolson, 'a typical naval officer, with all the habits of duty and discipline, of obedience and command, which the profession of seaman necessarily included'. He was ignorant of political matters, and quite unprepared for the unprecedented clash between the two Houses of Parliament which confronted him. His father had not informed him of what was at stake, and his plight was not eased by the often contradictory advice he received from his Secretaries, Lord Knollys and Sir Arthur Bigge. He was therefore profoundly grateful when Asquith told him that he would be prepared to come to an arrangement with the Leader of the Opposition over the Parliament Bill. This was consistent with Asquith's aim of keeping the Crown as far as possible out of the political arena.

The party truce lasted from May to November, during which time four representatives from each of the two major parties met on twenty-one occasions to find a solution to the constitutional deadlock. The failure of these conferences was due not to any basic differences over the theory of the constitution, although these existed, nor to any serious personal differences between the representatives. The conferences failed because the Unionists feared that reform of the Lords would inevitably lead to Home Rule. Lord Lansdowne, who dominated the Unionist side of the negotiations and who owned large estates in Southern Ireland, was unwilling to make the slightest concession to Home Rule. By November 1910 the party talks had broken down.

Asquith now had little alternative but to resume the attack on the Lords, and to ask King George for the 'guarantees' which he had failed to receive from King Edward before he died. These would be of vital importance in breaking the power of the Lords, and must be secured before another election was held. George V was unwilling to comply with his request, and Asquith found himself under pressure from members of his Cabinet to take a firmer line with the King. It was an unfortunate impasse, which was resolved only by the intervention of the King's Secretary, Lord Knollys. In December 1909, as Secretary to King Edward, he had advised his monarch against giving Asquith the 'guarantees'. On 29 April 1910 he had represented the King at a secret conference called at Lambeth Palace to discuss the political situation now that the Budget had been passed. Balfour had been present, and had indicated his willingness to form a government should the Liberals resign over the King's failure to give them the 'guarantees'. Edward VII had died a week after this meeting, and neither he nor Knollys had communicated this information to the new King. Knollys broke the November deadlock between the King and his Ministers by assuring George that in any event Balfour would decline to form an administration, once again remaining silent on what he knew of Balfour's intentions the previous April. It is not known why Knollys chose to act as he did, but it must be admitted that he advised the more prudent and expedient course and spared the Crown the charge of favouring the Unionists, the minority party. Thus on Knollys' advice, the King reluctantly agreed on 16 November to an immediate dissolution of Parliament and to a secret undertaking that he would create sufficient new Liberal peers to facilitate the passage of the Parliament Bill through the Lords.

Secure in the promise of 'guarantees' from the King, Asquith decided to put the issue of Lords reform before the nation. He announced that Parliament would be dissolved on 28 November. Before Parliament broke up, the Lords had debated alternative reform proposals put forward by Lansdowne, having first moved the postponement of the second reading of the Parliament Bill. The election was dull, even though Lloyd George attempted to focus public attention on the Lords. 'An aristocracy', he said, 'is like cheese; the older it is the higher it becomes.' The general public had, however, lost interest in the Lords, partly because the issue had faded out of public notice during the long party truce in the summer, and partly because the constitutional questions at stake were difficult for ordinary people to understand. Furthermore, this was the second election within twelve months and many electors just could not be bothered to vote. In fact, one in six of those who had voted earlier in the year did not do so on this occasion: the total vote fell by over a million. The result was almost identical with that in January, though a small turnover in seats had taken place. Liberals and Unionists had each won 272 seats, the Irish Nationalists 84, and Labour 42. It was a result which should have removed the King's doubts, stiffened Government resolve to press ahead with reform of the Lords, and persuaded the Unionist leadership that the time had come to retreat.

The Unionists were, however, unrepentant and decided to continue the struggle over the Parliament Bill, leaving the Government no alternative but to proceed with the Bill with the threat of creating enough Liberal peers for it to pass. Balfour and Lansdowne still did not know of George V's promise of 'guarantees', and believed that the Government were bluffing when they threatened to use the royal prerogative against them. By continuing resistance, they were getting themselves into a position from which it would be impossible to retreat.

The Parliament Bill was reintroduced in the Commons on 21 February 1911, and, after 900 keenly fought amendments, passed its third reading on 15 May. On 23 May it had its second reading in the Lords, and during the next six weeks they mutilated it by means of amendments. The Bill which the Commons had passed was transformed, but not rejected. It was nevertheless a challenge which the Government could not avoid. On 7 July the Opposition leaders were privately informed of George V's agreement to the creation of as many peers as were necessary for the passage of the Parliament Bill through a hostile House of Lords. It was only now that Balfour and Lansdowne saw that they had been outmanoeuvred, and that the time had come for them to surrender.

The outcome of the constitutional crisis thus hinged on whether Balfour and Lansdowne could persuade sufficient Unionist peers to vote with the Government and thus rescue the Crown from having to use its prerogative power. It was too late: they no longer retained the confidence of the Unionist party. This was apparent when Balfour met the Shadow Cabinet on the morning of 21 July and advised surrender. Although they voted with him, it was clear that they were deeply divided. Lansdowne failed to convince a meeting of over 200 Unionist peers that they must let the Bill pass. The Unionist party had split into two factions: the 'Hedgers', led by Lord Curzon, who were prepared to surrender, and the 'Ditchers', led by Lords Halsbury and Willoughby de Broke, who were prepared to continue their resistance to the Bill. The 'Ditchers' were clearly in the majority, and they had snatched the initiative from the party leaders. Balfour privately described the 'Ditcher' resistance as being fit only 'for music-hall consumption', but did very little to curtail their activities. 'Hedgers' and 'Ditchers' canvassed their fellow peers for support in the vote on the third reading of the Bill in the Lords. Asquith meanwhile indicated to the Opposition leaders that there would be no creation of peers until *after* the Lords had rejected the Bill, again showing his natural reluctance at having to take the unprecedented step of swamping the Lords with new creations. He had, however, drawn up a list (since published) of names of 249 men of Liberal convictions whom he was prepared to ennoble should the need arise.

The political atmosphere in the last days of July and early August was tense and unpleasant. It was generally accepted that the Government would be defeated on the third reading of the Parliament Bill in the Lords. The debate on the Commons' amendments to the Bill opened in the Lords on 9 August. The majority of speeches favoured rejection; Lansdowne counselled abstention. The debate was adjourned on the night of 9 August, and negotiations began between Lord Morley, the Liberal leader in the Lords, and Bigge, the King's Secretary, to dispel once and for all the illusion that the King would not use his prerogative. When the debate reopened on 10 August, Morley read out a statement asserting the King's willingness to create sufficient peers to pass the Parliament Bill. Morley read it a second time, adding, 'That, I think, is pretty conclusive.' A division was taken at 10.45 p.m. No one knew who would win. The tension was unbearable, and the result a surprise. The Government had a majority of 17; 37 Unionists and 13 bishops had voted with the 81 Liberal peers.

With the successful passage of the Parliament Bill, a creation of peers was no longer necessary. That night King George wrote in his diary, '. . . . so the Halsburyites were thank God beaten! It is indeed a great relief to me and I am spared any further humiliation by a creation of peers.' The Crown had survived a major constitutional crisis. King Edward can take little credit for this. His efforts as mediator had been only moderately successful, and he had occasionally been seriously out of touch with what his ministers were trying to do. It was perhaps his more inexperienced successor, George V, who emerged from this, the first serious political crisis of the reign, with his personal standing enhanced, if only because he had listened to the good sense of Knollys rather than to the unwise advice of Bigge. By giving Asquith the 'guarantees' requested in November 1910, George had rescued the Crown from a delicate predicament.

The Parliament Act of 1911 was perhaps the most significant constitutional reform since the 1867 Reform Act, and under it, the Lords' absolute veto over legislation had been transformed into a suspensory veto of two years' duration. The Upper House was henceforth impotent in financial matters. The life of Parliament was reduced from seven to five years. In addition, on 10 August 1911, the Commons had voted a Resolution for the payment of M.P.s on the basis of £400 a year for all members. The Parliament Act was a triumph for the forces of democracy. The wishes of an elected majority in the Lower House could now only be denied for a limited period. The radical reforms promised in 1906 and subsequently obstructed by the Lords could at last be achieved.

The victory over the Unionist peers was the greatest political achievement of the Liberal government since taking office in 1905. Asquith's authoritative and determined leadership had been outstanding. He had been at the height of his powers during the crisis, apart from his inactivity between January and April 1910, when he was feeling physically exhausted after a protracted election campaign. He had shown a high degree of political expertise throughout the crisis which had enabled him to carry his party and the majority of the British people with him. He had always treated Edward VII and George V with the utmost consideration. Lloyd George had been an admirable lieutenant, brilliantly taking the fight with the Lords to the country. Rarely in a long political career did his volatile genius and true Radical fervour show to greater effect than in this crisis. By their joint efforts Asquith and Lloyd George had revitalised the Liberal cause. Morale was buoyant: the party could now carry out its programme of Home Rule, disestablishment of the Welsh church, land reform, and social reform.

4 Anticlimax This Liberal achievement was, however, deceptive. The party had exhausted its radical energies in the struggle with the Lords, whereas the Unionists were still able to delay and to reject Liberal measures since their majority in the Upper House had not been changed by the Parliament Act. This vital question of the reform of the composition of the Lords had been postponed in 1911, mainly because the Liberals were unable to agree on an alternative to the hereditary principle, and were unwilling to tamper with the existing membership of the Upper House. They had no solution to the wider constitutional question of the exact role of a reformed Lords. Should it become a strong Second Chamber like the American Senate? Reforms since 1911 have reduced the suspensory veto to one year and have widened membership by the nomination of life peers, but they have failed to overcome the hostility of the Commons to any possibility of reform leading to a strong Second Chamber. The House of Lords still awaits its true reformation.

Defeat over the Parliament Act made the Unionist party more truculent than ever. Balfour was the first victim of increased militancy in the party, and a 'Balfour must go' campaign led to his resignation in November 1911. His successor was Bonar Law. This change in leadership signified an important stage in the development of the Unionist party. It marked the end of the era in which the party had been led by the landed classes, by men like Salisbury, Balfour and Lansdowne, who had had the time and the private income to play an active part in politics. The leadership of the party in the nineteenth century by representatives of the middle classes like Peel and Disraeli had been against the general trend of aristocratic leadership. The new generation of party leaders after 1911, Bonar Law, Stanley Baldwin and Neville Chamberlain, were businessmen with a more professional view of politics than their predecessors. Under the leadership of such men, the Unionist party redoubled its attempts to frustrate Liberal measures in and out of Parliament.

The constitutional crisis had revealed the Unionist party in an unfamiliar guise. The party which had for so long been regarded as the natural defender of the constitution had endangered it by unconstitutional behaviour. The Unionists' willingness to use direct action helped to undermine public respect for the conventional rules of political conduct. Liberal England in the years immediately preceding the Great War was torn by political violence bordering on civil war. Suffragettes, militant trade unionists, Ulstermen and Irish Nationalists were prepared to follow the Unionists' example by relying on force to gain their objectives.

Finally, the reduction of the Lords' powers precipitated the Ulster crisis (see Chapter VI). The Liberals were now free to introduce the Third Home Rule Bill in 1912 knowing that it would clear its major stumbling-block, the Lords, with a maximum delay of two years. The Unionists were, however, determined to prevent Home Rule at all costs, and their bigoted attitude encouraged Ulster's resistance to the point of civil war, which was only averted by the outbreak of the Great War in August 1914.

Chapter IV

Origins of the Welfare State 1906-14

1 The condition of the people—the Liberals and social reform The Liberals' concern with the 'condition of the people' question and the legislation they enacted not only helped to eliminate the archaic Victorian approach to social problems, but also pointed the way to the eventual solution. How and why did the party which had been most closely identified during the nineteenth century with the individualist philosophy and the belief in the minimum of state intervention as the best guarantee of liberty turn in the early twentieth century to a fundamentally opposite belief in increased state intervention as the best means of enlarging liberty?

England presented dramatic extremes of wealth and poverty in the Edwardian era. Just under half the national income went to about five millions of the working population, while the other fifteen million workers earned less than £160 per annum, the point at which income tax began. Almost one-third of the working classes lived in desperate poverty, their low wages failing to keep pace with the rising cost of living, and their existence made the more precarious by the constant threat of ill-health and unemployment.

Unfortunately the existing social services, embodied in the Poor Law Amendment Act of 1834, were totally inadequate. The framers of that statute had failed to unravel the fundamental causes of poverty. The 'workhouse test' was applied alike to able-bodied and sick, aged and children, and was resented by those sections of society it was designed to help. A contemporary observer noted that the new Poor Law 'did more to sour the hearts of the labouring population than did the privations consequent on all the actual poverty of the land'. The principles of 1834 harmonised with the Victorian reliance on laisser-faire, thrift, and self-help to solve social problems. In practice, however, the 'workhouse test' was often modified. Outdoor relief continued to be given to the sick, the elderly, and the unemployed, and workhouse children attended district schools. The 1870s saw a more humane interpretation of the regulations concerning the treatment of the poor in workhouses. For example, newly-created Poor Law hospitals, the forerunners of a public health service, were set up to take in the workhouse sick. Nevertheless, a strong conviction remained that the worker should help himself, but rarely was it asked whether the worker had sufficient wages to provide for himself. Private charity existed alongside the social services, but the efforts of associations like the Charity Organisation Society were limited by perennial shortages of funds.

Attitudes were, however, slowly changing. The second half of the nineteenth century witnessed a gradual revolution in social thinking which was to culminate in the Liberal reforms of 1906-14. The belief in self-reliance was being displaced by a belief in collective action for the relief of the less fortunate members of society. The trend towards collectivism had many disparate strands. The state was being compelled to intervene in order to secure at least minimum standards, not because of any ideological conviction, but merely to safeguard society as a whole. Protective legislation in the form of Drainage Acts, Mines Regulation Acts, Public Health Acts, Artisans' Dwellings Acts, Education Acts, were all being passed. As the orthodox *Economist* commented in 1895, 'Little by little and year by year, the fabric of State expenditure and State responsibility is built up like a coral island, cell on cell.' Thus a new conception of society, that of 'the Welfare State', began to take shape, something that Maurice Bruce has described as 'no more than the accumulation over many years of remedies to specific problems which in the end have reached such proportions as to create a new conception of governmental responsibility'. The revolution in social thinking in late Victorian

Britain was to some extent influenced by collectivist thinkers such as T. H. Green and the Fabians, but was, above all, the result of a new awareness of social problems created by statistics, reports, commissions, investigations, and surveys of one kind or another. The mountain of factual evidence that they presented was incontrovertible proof that the existing social services were inadequate and that urgent remedies were essential. The 'epoch-making' social investigations of Charles Booth into the *Life and Labour of the People in London* between 1886 and 1903, and of Seebohm Rowntree at York, *Poverty: a Study of Town Life*, published in 1901, provided indisputable evidence that probably more than a quarter of the population was living in poverty, that charity was insufficient, and that the community must intervene to help those who were incapable of helping themselves. The University Settlement movement brought many earnest young men (and future social reformers) like Beveridge, Morant, and Braithwaite to witness at first hand what life was like for the poor. The Boer War caused national alarm at the poor physical quality of recruits, and an Inter-departmental Committee on Physical Deterioration was set up in 1903-4 to investigate and propose remedies. The National Committee of Organised Labour on Old Age Pensions, backed by the T.U.C., the Co-operative Movement, and reformers like Reeves and Booth formed a powerful 'lobby', and successive Royal Commissions and Treasury Committees looked into the question.

Under the Unionist administration of 1900-5 no important social reforms were introduced. Joseph Chamberlain, one of its foremost members, had been interested in old age pensions since the 1890s, but he could neither persuade his party to bear the financial cost that pensions would impose, nor overcome the opposition to state-aided pensions from the influential Friendly Societies, which saw contributory state pensions as undesirable competition. Chamberlain's interest was side-tracked successively by the Boer War and Tariff Reform, and Unionist neglect left the field of social reform open for the Liberals.

The social reform issue had played little part in the Liberals' 1906 election campaign. There was no indication that the

Liberals were any more likely to grant old age pensions than the Unionists. The new Prime Minister, Campbell-Bannerman, who had a Gladstonian approach to social problems, was out of touch with the New Liberals, and had only tentatively included certain new radical ideas in the official Liberal programme between December 1904 and January 1906. His election address contained timid social ideas such as the relief of overcrowding, the 'colonisation' of the countryside, the improvement of the Poor Law, and measures to soften unemployment and alleviate the conditions of workers in sweated industries. Moreover, his promise of a massive reduction in public expenditure revealed his failure to appreciate the cost of social reform. The Premier represented powerful restraining forces in the Parliamentary Liberal Party. Although over half the Liberal members were new, they had wide experience of public life and were drawn from the commercial and professional middle-class. They belonged overwhelmingly to the Centre, for, as the Chief Whip, Herbert Gladstone, remarked to his leader early in 1906, 'There is no sign of any violent forward movement . . . The dangerous element does not amount to a dozen.'

This 'dangerous element' was indeed small in number, but its influence was decisive in committing the Liberal Party to a programme of social reform that would lead to a revolution in the Government's relations with its citizens. Lloyd George and Churchill were the leaders of the New Liberals, as the Radicals were called. Their views were a compound of personal concern at the plight of the 'left-out millions' and the political necessity for the Liberals to win working-class votes: the presence of a powerful Labour group in the Commons was a warning which astute politicians like Lloyd George and Churchill could not afford to ignore. The New Liberals believed in securing for all a minimum standard of living, in the words of Winston Churchill, 'a line below which we will not allow persons to live and labour, yet above which they may compete with the strength of their manhood'. Asquith, who became Prime Minister in 1908, shared this New Liberal vision, and gave invaluable encouragement to his more radical colleagues in the Cabinet in their attempts to achieve social reform. Extensive pressure for the New Liberalism was exerted from below by a group of highly influential individuals. Junior ministers like Charles Masterman; the journalists on *The Nation* newspaper, H. W. Massingham, H. N. Brailsford, L. T. Hobhouse, J. A. Hobson; social reformers like the Webbs; civil servants like Morant and Beveridge; the Christian Social Union; all helped in spreading the new ideas and in producing the conviction that state action was imperative. Lloyd George outlined the broad principles now underlying the policy of the Government in a speech at Swansea on October 1908: 'It has not abandoned the traditional ambition of the Liberal party to establish freedom and equality; but side by side with this effort it promotes measures for ameliorating the conditions of life for the multitude ... The old Liberals in this country used the natural discontent of the people with the poverty and precariousness of the means of subsistence as a motive power to win for them a better, more influential, and more honourable status in the citizenship of their native land. The new Liberalism, while pursuing this great political ideal with unflinching energy, devotes a part of its endeavour to the removing of the immediate causes of discontent. It is true that man cannot live by bread alone. It is equally true that a man cannot live without bread. Let Liberalism proceed with its glorious work of building up the temple of liberty in this country, but let it also bear in mind that the worshippers at that shrine have to live.'

2 Liberal reforms: helping the young and the old   Campbell-Bannerman's premiership (1905-8) proved to be relatively barren of social reform. His negative approach was designed to preserve party unity at the expense of controversial social reforms, but, in spite of this, some significant reforms were passed. Professor Bentley B. Gilbert, a leading American authority on the British social services, has claimed that 'the passage of the Education (Provision of Meals) Act of 1906 and the Education (Administrative Provisions) Act of 1907, establishing medical inspection in State schools, marks the beginning of the construction of the welfare state'. This may be so, but it is also clear that these two Acts were the product of a long-standing concern for children's welfare and an extension of legalised services that were already being provided by some local authorities.

The national birth-rate had been dropping since the 1870s, when it stood at 35 per 1000, and by 1906 it was down to 26 per 1000. The widespread concern at the slackening of population increase encouraged the growth of the Maternity and Child Welfare Movement, with such reforms as the provision of milk, the use of health visitors, improved midwifery, and infant welfare centres. Although the Committee on Physical Deterioration had heightened alarm at the poor physical quality of recruits during the Boer War, it had failed to produce tangible results. The Unionists had not implemented the Committee's proposals of school meals and school medical inspection, nor did the new Liberal ministry. Sir Robert Morant, the Permanent Secretary at the Board of Education and the real head of English education until his promotion in 1911, wrote privately on 23 February 1906: 'I find that my President's mind is practically a blank on the subject . . . the Party is probably considerably divided.' It was, in fact, a private member's Bill for the feeding of school children by the local education authorities (L.E.A.s), sponsored by a new Labour M.P., William Wilson, that forced the Government's hand in 1906. Since it could not properly oppose the measure, the Government adopted it. The Act set up a semi-voluntary, semi-official system whereby the L.E.A.s could either continue to use the existing voluntary organisation or provide their own school meals at the cost of a halfpenny rate. By 1910, 96 authorities were levying rates for school meals, and over 9,000,000 meals were being provided each year. Since neither the voluntary societies nor the ratepayers could cope with the increasing demand for school meals, a further Act was introduced in 1914 which gave the Board of Education powers to compel L.E.A.s to provide school meals and authorised a regular Exchequer grant to help with the cost. By 1914, the school meals service was providing over 14,000,000 school meals a year for some 158 000 children, Saturdays and school holidays included.

The introduction of school medical inspection in 1907 was a further example of unpremeditated action which the Liberal Government was forced to take. The efforts of two Liberal M.P.s, H. J. Tennant and W. W. Rea, were responsible for the Government's introduction of its own measure in 1907, the Education (Administrative Provisions) Bill, providing medical inspection, which was to begin on 1 January 1908. The importance of the Bill lay in the vaguely-worded clause thirteen, which authorised 'arrangements . . . for attending to the health and physical condition of children educated in public elementary schools'. McKenna, the new President of the Board of Education, denied that the Bill intended medical treatment, but he was clearly deceived by Morant, his Permanent Secretary, who, influenced by the Webbs, wanted a Fabian-planned school medical service. Morant saw that medical treatment must follow inspection, and had deliberately buried his measure for the treatment of children (clause thirteen) in a mass of other details in the hope that it would be passed without debate. His ruse worked, revealing the enormous power that could be wielded by an energetic civil servant, armed with a coherent scheme and only loosely supervised by his political masters. *Board of Education Circular* 576 laid the regulations for inspection, while *Circular* 596 provided the charter for the school medical service. It urged L.E.A.s to make available means for medical treatment and suggested how they could provide it. Thus, by administrative order rather than by political decision, an important reform was contrived far from public attention and controversy. Consequently more and more L.E.A.s provided medical treatment in school clinics, and in 1912 Exchequer grants were given to those L.E.A.s doing most in the way of treatment.

Herbert Samuel, Under-Secretary at the Home Office, was responsible for the introduction of Borstals and the probation service in 1907. The following year, in response to growing concern from the N.S.P.C.C. and other interested organisations, he supervised the passage through the Commons of the Children Act, a huge consolidating measure, repealing no fewer than thirty-nine earlier laws and making some important changes.

It covered the legal rights of children, including such matters as the protection of infant life, parental neglect of medical treatment necessary for a child's well-being, and cruelty to children. Penalties were imposed for allowing children to beg or to smoke. There was to be special treatment for child offenders, with emphasis more on treatment and care than on punishment. Moreover, delinquent children would in future be tried in special juvenile courts; they would not be sent to prison, and remand homes were set up to detain them while they were awaiting trial.

The importance of school meals, medical inspection and treatment, and the 'Children's Charter', as the Children Act was called, lies in the fact that it marked a further blow to the old Liberal principle that each individual in a free society should be responsible for his own welfare. What was more surprising was that the hallowed laisser-faire approach crumbled without any resistance, while there was no real political debate as to whether or not welfare legislation was desirable. When the Unionists obstructed the Liberal reforms, they did so not because the measures transgressed the long-established principle of individual responsibility, but on the short-term tactic of making the Liberal proposals so ruinously expensive and difficult to administer that they would embarrass the Government and prevent it completing its programme.

The pace of reform quickened in 1908, when Campbell-Bannerman resigned and his successor, Asquith, promoted the leading reformers, Lloyd George and Churchill, to the Treasury and the Board of Trade respectively. The new Prime Minister was conscious of his supporters' frustration. For two years the Government had failed to make headway against an obdurate House of Lords, and their legislative record was meagre. Popular disillusionment was reflected in a series of by-election defeats in 1908. Asquith saw that his party needed to regain the initiative and revive waning support. An old age pensions scheme, which he had promised in 1906 and had been working on ever since, was the answer. Reduced naval spending created a budget surplus for 1907 and so Asquith could both reduce taxes and lay the foundations for an expensive social reform. In the 1907 Budget he had announced that he was proposing to set aside £2,250,000 for non-contributory old age pensions, but once he became Prime Minister, it was the duty of the new Chancellor, Lloyd George, to introduce the measure. The Liberal leaders emphasised that the Pensions Bill was only the first stage of a wider framework of old age security, but they had no precise idea how much their scheme would cost; Asquith estimated £6,000,000. The Bill, introduced in May 1908, received the royal assent in August. Payments would begin on 1 January 1909. A non-contributory old age pension would be paid to all persons over 70 whose income did not exceed £31 per annum. The full sum of 5/- per week would be paid to those with a maximum annual income of £21, but less, by weekly units of 1/-, for those with incomes between £21 and £31. Pensions would be paid out every Friday at Post Offices. Local pension committees would determine eligibility, and pensions were to be denied for two years after 1 January 1908 to any old person who had previously accepted poor relief or who had been in prison within the last ten years, or who had habitually failed to work. Although the scheme was attacked as insufficient from both sides of the Commons, it was warmly welcomed by the poor. The Government felt that it had gone as far as the financial position would allow, and Churchill admitted publicly, 'We have not pretended to carry the toiler on to dry land. What we have done is to strap a lifebelt around him.' Asquith had forecast that rather more than 500,000 people would apply for pensions in 1909: in fact, over 650,000 applied, a figure rising to over 970,000 by 1914. The cost rose correspondingly, from over £8,000,000 in 1909 to over £12,000,000 four years later. Although old age pensions practically eliminated outdoor relief to those over seventy, they led to only a small reduction in the numbers receiving indoor relief.

The Liberals' Pension Act opened a new chapter in the history of the community's care for its least fortunate members, and the ease with which it passed was in itself an indication of the recognition that the old Poor Law was inadequate and that a new solution was required. Bruce has observed that the Act introduced a new principle into social policy: 'Hitherto relief had been provided, as an act of grace, for all the needy from local funds and only after a test of destitution. Now for the first time payments were to be made, as of right, from national funds to a section of the needy, the elderly, within strict limitations of age and means, but with no test of actual destitution.' Moreover Lloyd George's controversial Budget of 1909, which helped to finance the pensions scheme, introduced the transfer of wealth by taxation for the benefit of the needy. This was the way in which future social reform was to be financed by the community. Although the constitutional crisis caused a hiatus in the Liberals' legislative programme between 1909 and 1911, social reform had by no means been exhausted.

3 The problems of the wage earners Winston Churchill is alleged to have voiced his initial disappointment on taking office at the Board of Trade: 'There is nothing to do here: Lloyd George has taken all the plums.' Nevertheless he rapidly made that department the hub of social reform. Although some historians, e.g. Robert Rhodes James, and some politicians, e.g. Charles Masterman, have cast doubts on Churchill's sincerity as a social reformer, it would appear from his early public speeches that his convictions were genuine, and that he had a deep-seated desire to create a new system of social organisation. Deeply impressed by Rowntree's study of 'Poverty', Churchill had shown his awareness of the 'condition of the people' when he declared, 'I see little glory in an Empire which can rule the waves and is unable to flush its own sewers.' When he joined the Liberal Party in 1904 he soon became a spokesman for the New Liberals. Writing an article entitled 'The Untrodden Field in Politics', in *The Nation* in March 1908, he concluded, 'From many quarters we may work towards the establishment of that National Minimum below which competition cannot be allowed, but above which it may continue healthy and free, to vivify and fertilise the world.'

The 'sweated labour' question soon engaged Churchill's attention. In certain occupations, unskilled workers, frequently Jewish migrants who had settled in East London, had been exploited. These workers, many of them women employed in dressmaking, laboured long hours for miserably low wages. There were no effective laws to maintain minimum wage rates and decent conditions of work. Reformers proposed a general minimum wage rate, and Churchill accepted it. His Act of 1909 set up trade boards consisting of equal numbers of employers, employed, and officials, for certain scheduled trades (tailoring, the manufacture of paper boxes, laces and chains). These boards were to fix minimum rates for time-work and piece-work, and employers who paid less than the minimum were to be fined. The Trade Boards Act was to be enforced by factory inspectors, and some 200,000 workers, of whom 140,000 were female, were included.

Churchill's greatest achievement as a social reformer lay in his response to the problem of unemployment, the root cause of so much social distress. The Unemployed Workmen Act of 1905, which the Liberals had renewed in 1906 and had supplied with a £200,000 Treasury grant, had failed to help the skilled worker who found himself temporarily out of work. On the contrary, it had been the underemployed and casually-employed workers in occupations that were notoriously irregular (labouring, building, engineering and shipbuilding) who had taken advantage of the scheme. The 1907-8 depression had caused unemployment to rise to 7.2 per cent (800,000) in 1908, the highest level since 1886. The Liberal Party was far from popular, and Churchill realised that something positive would have to be done to counter unemployment and prevent the permanent defection of working-class votes to Labour. He had himself long admired the efficiency of the social welfare system in Germany, which he extolled to Asquith in December 1908: 'I say—thrust a big slice of Bismarckianism over the whole underside of our industrial system, and await the consequences, whatever they may be, with a good conscience.'

His own views on unemployment owed much to his advisers at the Board of Trade, Sir Hubert Llewellyn-Smith, the Permanent Secretary, and W. H. Beveridge. Having spent some years in a University Settlement and then written leading articles on social problems for *The Morning Post*, Beveridge had been appointed by Churchill to the Board of Trade. His was to be one of the most important influences in the continuing development of the Welfare State in Britain. In 1909, he published *Unemployment: A Problem of Industry*, in which he argued that since men in regular work could not provide protection for themselves against the bad times (only one-third of the workers actually belonging to trade unions were insured), collective cover against unemployment could be more widely provided by the State. Unemployment insurance and labour exchanges were the answer. According to Beveridge, 'The Labour Exchange thus opens a way of "dispauperisation" more humane, less costly and more effective than that of the "workhouse test"—the way of making the finding of work easy instead of merely making relief hard.' There is evidence to suggest that Churchill may also have been influenced by the recommendations of the Poor Law Commission, which he had seen privately before their publication in 1909. The Commission had strongly favoured labour exchanges and a state-assisted unemployment insurance scheme, agreeing with Beveridge in suggesting more public works, proper industrial training for the young, and raising the school-leaving age to fifteen.

It was characteristic of Churchill that, having made up his mind that something should be done, he freely borrowed ideas, framed legislation, and set about selling his schemes to his colleagues and the general public. However, since Lloyd George had not yet formulated a way of dealing with health insurance and since Churchill felt that insurance for unemployment and health must be presented as a whole, he set aside his scheme of unemployment insurance, covering some three million persons, and suggested making a start with labour exchanges. Thus, in May 1909, Churchill introduced his Labour Exchange Bill, on which he and Beveridge had been working since the previous summer. The Commons was nearly empty for the debates on the Bill, and, apart from some tepid Labour criticism, there were no divisions before the Bill became law in September. The six-clause Act empowered the Board of Trade to establish and maintain labour exchanges in places that needed them and to make regulations for their management. Beveridge became Director of the new supervisory organisation. The exchanges supplied a service: they would tell 'workmen where not to go and where to go'. On 1 February 1910, 83 exchanges were opened, and by 1914 the number had risen to 430.

The unemployment insurance scheme was delayed for two years by the struggle over the 'People's Budget' and House of Lords reform. It was to form Part II of Lloyd George's National Insurance Bill, and Churchill and his advisers continued to plan the measure. Beveridge wrote of Churchill, 'How much the single personality of a single Minister in a few critical months may change the course of social legislation', and Churchill retained his interest in the scheme even after he had left the Board of Trade in 1910. He himself said, 'There is no proposal in the field of politics that I care more about than this great insurance scheme', and it was essentially his ideas that formed the basis of Lloyd George's Bill. The purpose of insurance was to protect a man against the risks of unemployment. As Churchill pointed out, 'We seek to substitute for the pressure of the forces of nature, operating by chance on individuals, the pressure of the laws of insurance, operating through averages with modifying and miti- gating effects in individual cases.' Unskilled workers were almost all uninsured and unprotected, while only one-tenth of the total trade union membership (some million and a half workers) had taken out insurance policies against unemployment. Over twenty-five per cent of the social benefit funds of trade unions were paid out to unemployed members—more than to those incapacitated by accidents or injuries. The value of the German system of compulsory insurance was evident, and Church- ill could see that a similar British scheme was practicable now that the labour exchanges were functioning and could determine effectively whether a workman was unemployed or not. Although the Minority Report of the Royal Commission on the Poor Laws, inspired by the Webbs, had urged non-contributory aid to the unemployed as the provision of 'an enforced minimum of civilised life', Churchill recognised that many members of his party were not yet prepared to finance welfare out of general taxation. Compulsory contributory insurance, encouraging thrift and limiting any further extension of bureaucracy, seemed the obvious solution.

The unemployment insurance clauses of Lloyd George's Bill received little public attention, and passed the Commons' Standing Committee in six sittings. It went into effect on 15 July 1912, when the payment of contributions began, and benefits became payable on 15 January 1913. The scheme was an experiment, initially narrow in coverage and dealing with a small group of industries that were susceptible to high unemployment. Some two and a quarter million men in the building, mechanical engineering, iron-founding, shipbuilding, vehicle construction, and saw-milling trades were compulsorily insured. The trade union practice of requiring unemployed members to 'sign on' was adopted, as was the German method of registering contributions in an 'unemployment book' kept by the employer. Trade unions and labour exchanges were to administer the insurance scheme. A weekly levy of 2½d each from employer and employee was raised (to which the state added a third of the total at the end of each year), and, in return, the insured worker would receive 7/- a week when unemployed, qualifying for one week of benefit for each five contributions he had paid. There would be a maximum limit of fifteen weeks' unemployment benefit in any year. In the opinion of Maurice Bruce, 'The benefits offered in 1911 were deliberately set low to discourage malingering, but, like old age pensions, were in any case not intended to provide more than a "lifebelt" to supplement other savings . . . Unemployment insurance was intended to do no more than, in Beveridge's phrase, to average a man's earnings between good and bad times, or, as Churchill put it, to pool his luck with that of his fellow workers. It was, in fact, essentially insurance, socially organised and socially supplemented to give the citizen some protection against the miseries of depression and the proved inadequacies of ad hoc relief.'

Only a tentative conclusion can be reached as to the efficacy of the measures taken in 1909-11 to solve the problem of unemployment, since they never had a chance of proving themselves under the economic conditions for which they were designed. The general prosperity and low unemployment (2.1 per cent) between 1912 and 1914, and the outbreak of the Great War upset all previous calculations. In August 1914, after twenty-five months of contributions, the insurance fund had a surplus of £3,185,000, and could have carried a far greater degree of unemployment than the 2,250,000 workers in the insured trades were likely to suffer. Professor Gilbert has concluded: 'Welfare legislation hitherto had concerned itself with the helpless, either at the beginning or at the end of life . . . Now the Crown provided permanent service agencies to which the mature workman might apply for aid and direction not only in emergency, but indeed to prevent emergency . . . A precedent had been set. The departure made to prevent distress during unemployment took the State beyond the area of social welfare and into the area of social service.'

4 Health insurance   David Lloyd George had become a social reformer as a result of his personal experiences rather than from any intellectual theorising. He saw social problems in human terms and was passionately convinced that the worst thing to do was to do nothing. He was determined, Dr. J. W. Derry tells us, 'to utilise the resources of government to raise the quality of life of the masses and to seek to prevent the worst evils which afflicted British society'. His interest in national health insurance sprang not from his awareness of the inadequacies of the British medical system, but primarily from his wish to improve the standard of living of the British people. The evil to be treated was pauperism, not sickness; the poor were a focus for disease among the general public. Thus his massive plan to establish health insurance for the working class was predominantly a social measure. Indeed he had wanted to supplement the pensions scheme, which he had piloted through the Commons, by some provision for widows and orphans of those who died prematurely and for those persons who became chronically ill or unfit for work before pension age. 'David Lloyd George's massive plan to provide medical care for the British worker', Professor Gilbert assures us, 'was beyond comparison the most expensive, the most ambitious, and the most controversial of the (Liberal) measures.' The 'Insurance against Loss of Health and for the Prevention and Cure of Sickness', as the National Insurance Act, Part I, was officially known, came to be the high-water mark of the Liberal social welfare programme.

Lloyd George was aware of the inadequate provision of medical care for the vast majority of the population. Voluntary hospitals, Poor Law infirmaries, provident dispensaries, and individual general practitioners supplied a largely unco-ordinated medical service, good in places, but generally inefficient and socially inequitable. There was a double standard of medicine, one for the rich and another for the poor; the hospital service could not expand rapidly enough to meet the demands of a growing population; the two major killers of the adult population, syphilis and tuberculosis, were scarcely treated. The health problem was further complicated by medical politics, by disputes between the friendly societies, who ran provident dispensaries and employed individual doctors for their members, and the medical profession, fighting against lay control and cut-throat competition for patients. It was clear that the state would have to intervene in order to improve the health of its citizens, but must take care lest it antagonise powerful interests in the existing health scheme.

Once Lloyd George had seen for himself the working of the German insurance system and had sent his officials to study it in more detail, he began to plan the British scheme in 1908 with Germany as his model. Ways and means of implementing the principle of health insurance would have to be found. The cost would be too great to be borne directly by the Exchequer, and some contributory scheme would have to be devised that would be compatible with the activities of friendly societies, industrial assurance companies, and trade unions, which had achieved a great deal in the field of health insurance. The planning of the health insurance Bill, for which there was no previous precedent, was an astounding achievement for those politicians (Lloyd George, Masterman, Dr. C. Addison) and civil servants (W. J.

Braithwaite, Morant, and others) who collaborated on it. Braithwaite, who was Lloyd George's chief professional expert from December 1910 to December 1911 and the only adviser with personal experience of insurance, must be regarded as the main architect of the scheme. In two and a half months, between the middle of February and the end of April 1911, most of the health clauses of the Bill took shape. Lloyd George's powers of management, improvisation and compromise were tested to the full as he found his way round the almost insuperable difficulties and opposition that confronted him from the conception to the execution of the measure. He introduced his proposals to the Commons on 4 May 1911. A compulsory weekly insurance levy against loss of health at the rate of 4d per employee, 3d per employer, and 2d from the state was imposed on all workers earning less than £160 a year and on all manual labourers between the ages of 16 and 60. In return, the insured worker received as benefits medical treatment from a general practitioner with free medicine, sickness benefit of 10/- a week for 13 weeks and 5/- a week for the next 13 weeks to begin on the fourth day of illness, 5/- a week disability benefit, maternity benefit of 30/-, and the right to treatment in a sanatorium. A grant of £1,500,000 was given for the provision of sanatoria, while 1d per insured head was allowed for research, thus making possible the foundation of the Medical Research Council. The payment of benefits was entrusted to the 'approved societies', a status accorded to friendly societies, trade unions, and insurance companies to enable them to participate in the scheme, while medical care was supervised by local Insurance Committees.

Although the Unionists endeavoured to exploit opposition to the Bill, it was in fact backstairs 'lobby' activity that caused Lloyd George more difficulty than the formal political debate in Westminster. With the support of Labour members assured by the promise of payment of M.P.s, and with the use of the closure, Lloyd George's Bill received the royal assent on 16 December 1911. Moreover, through his persuasive charm he had dispelled the doubts of the friendly societies, and, knowing how and when to yield to the more powerful pressure groups (the industrial assurance companies and trade unions) he had agreed to make them 'approved societies', which would enable them to help administer his scheme. Health insurance then came under attack from various directions. The Government's defeat in the Oldham by-election in November 1911 was attributed to the unpopularity of the National Insurance Bill; it was clear that national insurance, unlike old age pensions, was unpopular with the working classes, who, besides being fundamentally suspicious of any further increase in the activities of the state, resented the compulsory health contribution. The Harmsworth Press launched a frenzied campaign against health insurance, and there were demonstrations at the Albert Hall when titled ladies and their domestic servants protested at being made to lick stamps! A much more serious challenge to the effective working of the Act came from the medical profession, who revolted against the terms of service offered. The British Medical Association broke off negotiations with Lloyd George, who, by giving in to the doctors' demands, succeeded in appeasing a majority of them. Nearly 15,000 doctors had signed contracts with the insurance committees when the medical part of the insurance scheme came into effect in January 1913, and the doctors, with enhanced status and increased remuneration, were among its prime beneficiaries. Practical difficulties were also overcome. Administrative machinery, departmental regulations, premises, staff, all had to be acquired and set in motion before July 1912. The National Health Insurance Committee, with Masterman as chairman and Morant as chief civil servant, supervised the establishment of the new service. Circulars were sent out, cards printed, stamps put on sale and contributions collected on 15 July, the starting date. Many details remained, and in 1913 an Amending Act was passed to give statutory authority for a 2/6 rise in medical benefit which Lloyd George had promised in 1912, and to remove anomalies and injustices in the administration of health insurance. Further improvements were being contemplated when War intervened. By 1914, thirteen million people were insured.

The health insurance scheme was a massive achievement, the most ambitious example to date of the state taking on a new function of government, providing for the citizen what the citizen was unwilling, or unable, to provide for himself. The importance of health insurance was not that it was an alternative to poor law medical facilities but rather that it enabled the British working class to avoid the poor law and pauperism altogether. Lloyd George had constructed a plan to supply medical care for the British worker on a much larger scale than the German scheme, covering more people and giving greater benefits. The insurance contributions of worker, employer and the state provided the financial resources for a 'reasonably adequate' system of benefits and treatment. However, national health insurance did not create a new national health service. There was not even a single Ministry of Health. Control over the nation's health was rigidly divided between the Local Government Board and the Insurance Commissions. The scheme was essentially an organisation for sickness insurance rather than for the positive encouragement of health. Future reformers of the health service would retain the principle of insurance, but would reject the cumbersome system of administration through the powerful private insurance agencies which Lloyd George had had to appease by inclusion in his Act.

The institution of pensions and social insurance had been a stupendous achievement by the Liberal Government. A handful of enterprising reformers, uncertain of what they were doing and yet convinced that it needed to be done, had overcome great administrative difficulties and had taken the state 'into an entirely new field of activity and although by no means solving the problem of the condition of the people, they settled the lines upon which the eventual solution would be found'. Their reforms were important for several reasons. They had helped to bring about a change of attitude in regard to social problems. The moral disgrace that was attached to poverty was being replaced by social concern about the poor. Moreover, although the objects of Liberal social policy were palliative rather than preventative, they did initiate a new sense of social responsibility and a new kind of welfare machinery, the future promise of which was greater than its present attainment. Their use of the principle of insurance against ill-health and unemployment, together with the social agencies such as labour exchanges and the free medical system, laid the foundations of the modern welfare state. When economic catastrophe and social hardship struck Britain in the 1920s and 1930s, the real significance of the Liberal achievement could be appreciated. When mass unemployment came, only a small legislative amendment was sufficient to widen Churchill's unemployment insurance scheme to cover all industrial workers, and a nation-wide system of unemployment benefits and labour exchanges was in being to blunt the edge of starvation and prevent distress turning to political violence. Furthermore, the success of the Labour party in extending the welfare services after 1945 was similarly dependent on what the Liberals had achieved before 1914.

The Liberals' performance in political terms was equally remarkable. Without any major party upset, the vast majority of Liberal M.P.s acquiesced in the views of the small minority of New Liberals that the party's traditional respect for the freedom of the individual must be tempered by a degree of collective control for those unable to help themselves. The other parties had accepted, without providing any real opposition to it, the Liberals' belief that insurance was the best way of providing state benefits. The Unionists totally failed to raise the question whether the principle of insurance was a good or a bad thing for the British people. Some Labour M.P.s, led by Philip Snowden, had insisted that the only socialist way of providing state benefits was through general taxation graduated according to the individual's ability to pay. Ramsay MacDonald was, however, so anxious to secure Liberal help in reversing the Osborne judgement that he pledged Labour support to Lloyd George's National Insurance Bill. Henceforth the Labour party was to accept the principle of insurance as the established method of extending the welfare state.

G. D. H. Cole and Raymond Postgate have suggested that the Liberal reforms were essentially a conservative measure aimed at preserving the existing economic order against socialist attack, and that the cost of the new health and unemployment service established under the National Insurance Act, so far from effecting a transfer of wealth, fell on the workers themselves. This is an interesting point of view, but unreasonable since the Liberals, working with limited funds and facing severe political difficulties, were forced to adopt a realistic approach. Something had to be done, and social insurance was the way to do it. Half a loaf was surely better than no loaf at all. In the end, baulked by the outbreak of war from further reforms and destroyed as a political force soon after the war ended, the Liberal party had nonetheless left a memorial that time would not deface—the Welfare State.

Chapter V

The Irish Question re-opened

1 Ireland 1886-1910 After the two elections in 1910 and the passage of the Parliament Act, Home Rule for Ireland was once again to dominate the political scene. It would at last be possible for a Home Rule Bill to become law two years after its introduction into the Commons. However, the Unionist party, seizing on the grievances of the loyalist Protestant province of Ulster, were to take the issue out of the parliamentary arena and make an open appeal to force. The Liberal Government, on the other hand, preferring to put their faith in the well-tried conventions of British Parliamentary democracy, were unable to check, and indeed accelerated, the remorseless drift towards civil war which resulted. The crisis in Ireland was the most serious challenge to the authority of the Liberals, and their most lamentable failure.

Gladstone had been unable to get Parliament to pass Home Rule in 1886 and in 1893. Recognising that he was beaten, he did not resign and did not dissolve Parliament. Instead Home Rule was shelved by the Liberal party. In 1890, Parnell's political career had been ruined after the O'Shea divorce action. His powerful party had split into two warring factions, severely damaging the Nationalist cause. Parnell's refusal to relinquish power had shaken the alliance between the Irish party and the Liberals, while the Catholic hierarchy's disapproval of his behaviour had helped to discredit the Home Rule movement in Ireland. In Britain, the public was more interested in foreign and imperial adventures, and twenty years were to pass before the Irish problem again attracted attention.

Unionist governments, with the exception of the Liberal interlude between 1892 and 1895, held power from 1886 to 1905. As the party of the Empire and of the 'Protestant Ascendancy' in Ireland, the Unionists were opposed to the notion of a separate Irish parliament in which the traditional rulers would be replaced by a Roman Catholic ascendancy. Lord Salisbury, the Unionist Prime Minister, ignored the Home Rule issue and applied a policy of firm government of Ireland, tempered by social and economic reforms which, he hoped, would eliminate those grievances which had nourished the Home Rule movement. Arthur Balfour, first as Chief Secretary and later as Prime Minister, was the main architect of this Unionist policy of 'Killing Home Rule by Kindness'. On his arrival in Ireland early in 1887, he had encountered a renewed form of land war, the 'Plan of Campaign', organised by John Dillon and the National league to protect tenants evicted for rent arrears. This movement was enjoying rapid success, and Balfour reacted to the situation with a harsh Crimes Act in July 1887 which gave him far-reaching powers to deal with land agitation. By 1890, the 'Plan of Campaign', lacking the open support of Parnell and crippled by acute shortage of money, had been crushed. The ringleaders were imprisoned and law and order restored. The Crimes Act became a permanent feature of the Irish legal code and remained on the statute books until 1907.

At the same time, however, Balfour's administration had begun to implement important social reforms. Balfour believed that the essential grievance of the Irish people centred on the question of land ownership: a small Anglo-Irish Protestant class owned vast estates, while the mass of native Catholic peasantry existed on tiny holdings under an unjust system of land tenure. Gladstone's Land Acts had reduced, but had not solved this problem. Balfour aimed to eliminate the evils of landlordism altogether, and at the same time to obtain fair compensation for the landlords, who formed a powerful section of the Unionist party.

Balfour showed his willingness to engage in land reform by an act of 1887 which revised in the tenants' favour the 'judicial rents' fixed under Gladstone's act of 1881. Ashbourne's Act of

1885 had initiated a limited scheme of land purchase, aiming to transfer ownership of land from the existing owners to the tenants, with the British government providing the necessary financial support. By Acts of 1888, 1891 and 1896, Balfour extended this scheme, making the terms of land purchase more attractive. Wyndham's Act of 1903 offered terms that were acceptable to landlord and tenant alike, so that the land purchase scheme, which was still optional, was almost universally put into operation. The British government was willing to provide more money than before to ensure success. They hoped to encourage landlords to sell entire estates by allowing them to charge higher prices for their land and by paying them in cash. In this way more land was made available for tenant purchase and for redistribution to the landless. Prospective tenant purchasers were helped by reduced rates of interest on loans and by an extended repayment period. They could now buy their land on very reasonable terms—yearly payments of $3\frac{1}{4}$ per cent spread over a period of 68 years. The scheme was undoubtedly successful: although in 1903 there were still more than 500,000 tenant farmers, by 1909 over 270,000 purchases had been arranged and a further 46,000 were being negotiated. The deep-rooted problem of landlordism had been largely overcome to the mutual satisfaction of all concerned.

Concurrent with these social reforms were a number of important economic measures to combat the effects of the agricultural depression caused by increasing overseas competition. Ireland, with its predominantly agricultural economy, was particularly hard hit. In 1891 Congested District Boards had been set up to administer public assistance to areas of exceptional poverty, and to improve agriculture and local industries. These Boards later took advantage of powers given them under Wyndham's Act to purchase over 2,000,000 acres of untenanted land, which was then redistributed among the landless peasants. Irish agriculture was improved by the spread of co-operative farming. By 1904 some 800 local co-operatives were selling their produce in large quantities. A leading Irish Unionist, Horace Plunkett, who had pioneered the adoption of the co-operative idea in Ireland, was appointed President of the Department of Agriculture and Technical Instruction for Ireland, set up by the Government in 1899 to improve the standard of farming. These Unionist reforms helped to bring relative prosperity and political quiet.

In 1898 the Unionists had passed a Local Government (Ireland) Act, providing for local councils and poor law guardians elected on the English model. Beyond this the Unionists would not go. A scheme of 'devolution', whereby a central Irish council would exercise some local authority within the framework of the existing constitution, was unofficially devised and discussed in 1904-5 by Lord Dunraven and Sir Anthony MacDonnell, Under-Secretary at Dublin Castle, but the proposals went too far for most Unionists; the Chief Secretary, George Wyndham, was dismissed and the scheme was subsequently a factor in Balfour's resignation in December 1905.

Balfour had relinquished office hoping that as soon as the Liberals had to shape a policy of their own sharp differences would appear among them. Campbell-Bannerman and the Roseberyite faction seemed at loggerheads over Home Rule. However, at Stirling on 23 November 1905, Campbell-Bannerman had, with the prior agreement of Rosebery's supposed colleagues, Asquith, Grey and Haldane, put forward the formula that the Liberal party should go to the polls with a 'step by step' approach towards Home Rule. Campbell-Bannerman thus united the Liberal factions, except for Rosebery, and Home Rule played little part in the election campaign. Moreover, the prospects for Home Rule in the near future were not enhanced by the Liberals' victory. With their commanding overall majority they were no longer dependent on Irish votes nor inclined to commit the party's fortunes to the vicissitudes of the Irish question. Irish affairs were delegated to the Chief Secretaries, Bryce (until 1906) and Birrell, who was to retain the office until 1916. Augustine Birrell, a witty man of letters, sympathetic to Irish demands and initially popular with the Irish leaders, was a political lightweight. He lacked real insight into the Irish problem, and his complacency and incompetence in administration were major reasons for the Liberals' losing control of Ireland in the pre-war years.

The Government revived the 'devolution' scheme of 1904-5 and embodied it in the Irish Council Bill, 1907, but Unionist opposition forced it to be abandoned. John Redmond, the Nationalist leader, was disconcerted by the Liberals' failure to proceed towards Home Rule. Redmond had headed the 'Parnellite' faction after 1891, and had become chairman of the reunited party in 1900. His political ability, fine presence, and powers of oratory made him an admirable and dignified parliamentary leader. Redmond believed in the supremacy of the British Parliament and in the attainment of Home Rule by constitutional means. His moderation contrasted sharply with the new extremist nationalist forces that had been growing in Ireland during the nineties. Fenianism had revived, and in 1898 Arthur Griffith, a Dublin printer, founded a weekly paper, the *United Irishman*, in which he put forward the doctrine of 'Sinn Fein' ('ourselves alone'), advocating non-cooperation with Britain. In addition, James Connolly, the founder of the Irish Socialist Republican party, began to publish the *Workers' Republic* to agitate for a Socialist Ireland freed from British rule. Off the political stage, there was a simultaneous upsurge of romantic interest in Ireland's past. Both the Gaelic Athletic Association (which encouraged Irish sports), and the Gaelic League (which revived the general use of the Irish language) thrived, while a group of talented Anglo-Irish writers and dramatists sought to develop a distinctly national literature. Although this Gaelic revival was apolitical in origin, it undoubtedly had political repercussions which worked in favour of breaking the union with Britain. Fanned by these separate movements and by the Irish Republican Brotherhood, a more militant nationalism flourished than Redmond and his parliamentary colleagues realised. 'Ulster is Ireland's,' was the comment of *Irish Freedom*, 'and shall remain Ireland's. We will fight them (i.e. the Ulster Unionists) if they want fighting, but we will never let them go, never.' Redmond was increasingly to run the risk of weakening his authority in Ireland by his policy of co-operation with the Liberal government. His career was to end in personal tragedy. How could a moderate, who believed in democratic methods, hope to achieve his ends in a situation where extremism and the use of force were increasingly favoured?

For the time being, however, Redmond found himself in a much stronger bargaining position after the General Elections of 1910 had once again made a Liberal government dependent on Nationalist votes. The Liberals, elated by the successful granting of self-government to the Boer Republics in South Africa and admiring Redmond's responsible attitude, considered Home Rule to be a more practical proposition than it had been for many years. It had been official party policy for the 1910 elections. The passage of the Parliament Act in the autumn of 1911 prepared the way for the realisation of Home Rule by constitutional means. At this point, however, moderate Nationalist and Liberal hopes were shattered by open rebellion in Ulster.

2 The Ulster question   Professor Mansergh in his lucid study of the Irish question has observed that 'if the Ulster Question were not one of the tragedies of history, it might well be regarded as one of the more remarkable of its curiosities'. The reason for Ulster's isolation in a country which forms so natural a geographic unit can be traced back to the English conquest of Ireland. Behind a formidable frontier of mountains and lakes, the nine counties of Ulster had been the last stronghold of Gaelic Ireland to be conquered in 1603. When the rebellious Earls of Tyrone and Tyrconnel fled to the continent in 1607, James I confiscated the province and began the 'Plantation' of Ulster. The early Stuarts sought to Anglicise the province by encouraging large-scale English and Scottish colonisation with grants of land. The settlers brought their own farming methods, social customs, and Protestant beliefs. Ireland was still a predominantly Catholic country, but the Presbyterian Scots gave Ulster a religion that was different from that of the rest of Ireland. Within a generation of the 'plantations', the socio-economic and religious demarcations that were to divide Ulster from the other provinces had already taken shape, and they were irrevocably underlined by the events of 1689-90. Although William of Orange deposed James II as King of England in 1689, James continued his resistance in

Ireland, supported by the great majority of his Irish Catholic subjects. On 1 July 1690, William III's large army decisively defeated James's forces on the line of the River Boyne. The memory of that event has lasted in Irish politics to the present day, 'for', as Professor Beckett says, 'the Boyne was the critical moment of a long struggle between the Roman Catholic and Protestant interests'. (*A Short History of Ireland*, Hutchinson, 1952.) The Protestant Ascendancy in Ireland had been secured.

The Act of Union (1800) through its economic and religious consequences further emphasised the development of two separate cultures in Ireland. Whereas the phenomenal growth of Belfast in the early nineteenth century from market town to modern industrial port helped to link Ulster with the spreading Industrial Revolution, the rest of Ireland did not enjoy similar economic benefits from the Union. Religious rivalries in Ulster were intensified by the granting of Catholic Emancipation, by the migration of Catholics into the North in search of employment, and by the land hunger caused by a rapidly increasing population. By 1850, thirty-five per cent of the province were Catholics, scattered throughout the nine counties. An inadequate education system and unenlightened political leadership could do nothing to soothe the religious passion which now permeated Ulster's society and politics. The predominant mood of nineteenth-century Belfast was very accurately caught by a contemporary, Lord Morley, in his *Recollections*. 'Strange to say', he wrote, 'this great and flourishing community where energy, intelligence and enterprise have achieved results so striking, has proved to harbour a spirit of bigotry and violence for which a parallel can hardly be found in any town in Western Europe.'

Gladstone's sudden conversion to Home Rule in 1886 had taken Ulster by surprise. Parnell and the Nationalists had deliberately sought to minimise the importance of Ulster's rights, believing that Ireland was one nation, and within that nation the will of the majority would, and should, prevail. Gladstone regarded the large Nationalist majority at Westminster as truly representative of 'the voice of Ireland'. He was prepared to examine any practicable scheme of exclusion for Ulster, but since nothing that to him appeared practicable was proposed, his two Home Rule Bills took no account of Ulster's special case. This was a disastrous oversight, since it reinforced the worst fears of Ulster Protestants about the kind of treatment they could expect from the Liberal-Nationalist alliance. They declared that Home Rule in the form of a Dublin Parliament would be 'Rome Rule'. The political parties now followed religious alignments. From 1886 onwards, all Protestants voted Unionist, while Catholics voted Nationalist. Protestant Ulster mobilised to fight Home Rule, and the fanatically sectarian Orange Order, founded in 1795 to perpetuate the 'pious and immortal memory' of William III, became a politically respectable and powerful organisation for the continuation of the Union. The Ulster Defence Union kept alive the spirit of resistance to Home Rule between 1886 and 1910, and in addition the Ulster Unionist Council was founded in 1905 as a highly influential central Unionist authority in the province.

The revival of Home Rule after the events of 1909-11 made the Ulster Unionists even more resolute. In February 1910, Sir Edward Carson, a Dublin Protestant and a famous advocate who had held office under the Unionists, was appointed leader. Carson was a complex personality. He had a Cromwellian touch about him; outwardly he was a strong man, austere, determined, fanatical, and unbending, but, in private, he was very different, for he despised religious intolerance and was willing to negotiate. One major reason for his success at the Bar lay in the fact that he believed so fervently in the justice of his case and could make others believe in it too. This was the special quality that Carson contributed to Ulster's fight. His dominant political belief had long been the maintenance of the Union between Great Britain and Ireland, since he was convinced that Ireland could not survive without it. He had first taken up the Ulster cause as the most effective way of destroying Home Rule and keeping all Ireland in the Union, but soon became totally involved in maintaining Ulster's special position for its own sake. He saw that he must act as the uncompromising spokesman of the Ulster people, and that the British government must be made to take Ulster's demands seriously. It was essential, therefore, that Ulster Protestants should be organised, disciplined, and prepared to resist should the Home Rule Bill become law. Carson wanted Ulster's resistance to be taken so seriously by the Liberal government that they would drop Home Rule altogether.

Was Carson bluffing, or would he really have carried out his threats had the First World War not intervened? Beckett, Mansergh and Stewart have argued that Carson's threats had some substance, that it was highly probable that Ulster would have resisted, and that its fight would have been successful. Dangerfield, however, believes that the pre-war Liberal government would have lacked the courage to coerce the Ulstermen. He adds moreover that Carson cherished hopes of high office in a future Unionist government and would not therefore have used force. Blake, while agreeing that the Ulstermen were in deadly earnest, doubted whether Carson himself, a lawyer and parliamentarian, was the man to violate the constitution. Blake concludes: 'Perhaps this was why in the last resort Asquith could not bring himself to take seriously the threats of someone whom he knew so well and with whom he had so often crossed swords in the law courts and the House of Commons.'

While Carson may or may not have been bluffing, there seems little doubt that his loyal henchman, Captain James Craig, would not have hesitated to take up arms against his King. A typical Ulsterman, Craig had had wide experience as businessman, soldier, and M.P., and his clear mind, calm disposition and remarkable powers of organisation were invaluable in mobilising Ulster for the struggle that lay ahead.

The wholehearted commitment of the Conservative and Unionist party to Ulster's resistance was another great asset. This support was of long standing, since the landed classes who had ruled Ireland for so long had been intimately connected with the English landed aristocracy. The landowners believed that Home Rule would weaken what was left of their political influence in Ireland, and would be followed by the expropriation of their Irish property. Furthermore, as the party of the Empire the Unionists believed that the Ulster loyalists should be free to retain the Union with Great Britain if they so wished. In 1886, having seen the electoral possibilities of defeating Home Rule by championing Ulster's rights, Lord Randolph Churchill had rightly prophesied that 'the Orange card would be the one to play'. In the event Home Rule had been defeated in 1886, and the defection of the Liberal Unionists into the ranks of the Conservative party had further strengthened its ties with Ulster.

Andrew Bonar Law, a comparative newcomer to the political scene, became Leader of the Unionist party in 1911. One can understand his reasons for pledging Unionist support to the Ulster cause. He had spent much of his childhood in Ulster, where his father had been a Presbyterian Minister, and he was thus personally involved. The Unionist party was divided and demoralised after its recent political humiliations; Ulster was an obvious rallying point. The Liberal government, by ignoring legitimate grievances, had committed a grave injustice against the Protestant inhabitants of Ulster. Bonar Law was not bigoted, but he was outraged that his Protestant fellow-countrymen should be forced to break the Union and submit to the wishes of their hereditary enemies in the Catholic South. Like Carson, Bonar Law advocated the use of force only because he knew it would never have to be used since the Liberals, whom he despised, would capitulate to Ulster's demands. Differing from extreme Unionists like Lord Lansdowne and Walter Long, he recognised that Home Rule would ultimately pass, provided an offer of exclusion acceptable to Ulster was first made.

While Bonar Law's views on Ulster were to some extent justifiable, his political tactics were not. The Unionists found themselves 'sick with office hunger' in 1911. They felt cheated by the alliance between the Government and Redmond, and frustrated by the prospect of permanent defeat in Parliament. After the passage of the Parliament Act, they had been deprived of their last hope of halting Home Rule by constitutional means. In their utter desperation, the Unionist leaders turned away from Parliament for a solution. Bonar Law intended to use the two years' breathing space of the Lords' veto to work for a dissolution of Parliament, confident that the Unionists would win the ensuing general election. At the same time, by focusing attention on Ulster's stand, he sought to convince the Government of the inadvisability of passing the Home Rule Bill.

Bonar Law's total attachment to Ulster's resistance was declared to a meeting of over 100,000 Ulster Unionists at Balmoral, a Belfast suburb, on 9 April 1912, on the eve of the publication of Asquith's Home Rule Bill. On 29 July he addressed a Unionist gathering at Blenheim, where his speech revealed the desperation and utter irresponsibility of Unionist policy. He described the Government as 'a Revolutionary Committee which has seized upon despotic power by fraud', and went on to exclaim 'There are things stronger than Parliamentary majorities'. He concluded by asserting that the Ulstermen 'would be justified in resisting ... by all means in their power, including force ... I can imagine no length of resistance to which Ulster can go in which I should not be prepared to support them, and in which, in my belief, they would not be supported by the overwhelming majority of the British people.' This speech achieved notoriety, and is interesting in that it reveals not only the contempt which the Unionists felt towards parliamentary democracy but also the extent to which they were prepared to defy the wishes of a democratically elected Government by an undisguised call for force. On the other side of the question Robert Blake, Bonar Law's biographer, supports Sir Robert Ensor's argument that it was the Liberals who had broken the democratic convention, for their Home Rule Bill ignored 'the deeper foundations on which alone democratic constitutionalism can rest—respect for minorities and for the subtle boundary which divides government by freedom and consent from that by dictatorship and violence'. This may be a valid point, but it cannot absolve the Unionist leaders from the charge of unconstitutional behaviour and of fomenting civil war in Ireland.

3 Government failures 1912-13 Asquith had never been a strong advocate of Home Rule, but his political dependence on Redmond's votes after the 1910 elections led him, like Gladstone before, to favour the Nationalists' argument that Ireland was one nation. (He perhaps overlooked the fact that Redmond was equally dependent on the Liberals continuing in office: a Unionist government would be a fatal prospect for Home Rule.) He therefore ignored the special claims of Ulster and refused to believe that the Ulster Protestants would carry out their threats of force. On 11 April 1912 he introduced his Home Rule Bill into the Commons. The Imperial Parliament at Westminster was to remain supreme 'over all persons, matters and things in Ireland', and to it forty-two Irish members would still be sent. Some degree of self-government under the Crown was offered to the new Dublin executive and parliament, which could make its own laws for peace, order and good government. As early as February 1912, Asquith had recognised that 'special treatment must be provided for the Ulster counties'. He was, however, unwilling to negotiate over Ulster unless forced to do so; the Bill made no arrangement for the exclusion of Ulster, even though it wished to remain under the British Parliament. The Bill was therefore immediately condemned by the Ulster Unionists. On 11 June 1912, Asquith failed to come to a compromise with Ulster, when he withheld support from the Agar-Robartes Amendment to exclude four Ulster counties from the operation of the Bill. Redmond refused to consider exclusion at any price, Asquith chose to 'wait and see', the Amendment was defeated, and a favourable opportunity was lost.

Asquith's handling of the crisis which followed in Ulster has caused controversy among historians. On the one hand there are the critical opinions of Ensor, Blake and Stewart, on the other the praise that Jenkins accords to Asquith's tactics of 'wait and see'. Asquith's defence must rest on the fact that the problems of Ulster were, and still appear to be, insoluble. Countless statesmen before and since have jeopardised their political reputations in the Irish imbroglio. Asquith was no exception to the rule. Even if he had accepted the principle of exclusion in the face of resolute opposition from the Nationalists and many members of his own party, how was Ulster to be defined? Only in four of the nine counties did the Protestants have a clear majority. Furthermore, such was the negative and irresponsible temper of the

Unionist party and its Ulster allies at the time that there was little hope that they would accept the exclusion of Ulster as a substitute for the total abandonment of Home Rule. In the event this proved to be the case. Even taking these nearly insuperable difficulties into account, however, Asquith's limitations cannot be denied. Confronted by an armed revolt in Ulster and the need for immediate action, Asquith procrastinated, failing to arrest those who were openly advocating sedition in Belfast (including the Leader of His Majesty's Opposition) and to suppress the private armies that were forming. His equivocal attitude and delayed concessions served only to encourage the forces of opposition in Ulster, disheartened Government supporters and made the situation more grim. Blake is very near the mark when he observes that 'Asquith was temperamentally a constitutionalist. He was deeply imbued with the tradition of Gladstonian Liberalism, the belief that all things can be settled within the framework of the constitution, that in the last resort a minority will always accept the decisions of a majority'. The failure of Asquith to overcome the opposition of a minority determined to resist the wishes of the majority was as much the failure of Liberalism in the fast-changing political climate before 1914. Ensor was perhaps being wise after the event when he wrote: 'A bolder course could have run straighter, and would have been at once more honourable and more helpful', but it is difficult not to agree with his conclusion that if Redmond had been able to represent to his people concession to Ulster as something which the government 'imposed on him against his will and without his acceptance, he might then have directed their minds to their true task—that of winning Ulster's eventual adhesion by consent'.

Consent to the Home Rule Bill was the last thing that the Unionists were prepared to give. The Bill was fiercely contested during its passage through the Commons and only passed in January 1913 because of the Government's ruthless use of the guillotine procedure. A fortnight later it was rejected by the Lords. In March 1913, the Bill was again introduced into the Commons and passed its second reading (this time there was no committee stage), but in July the Lords once again threw it out.

A number of unseemly incidents marred the dignity of Parliament, but Bonar Law did not disown the ill-mannered conduct of his supporters. Contemptuous of an institution in which it was doomed to failure, the Unionist party, which had prided itself as the party of law and order, now put its faith in mob rule.

In Ulster, Carson and Craig had resolved that there could be no turning back. At Craigavon on 23 September 1911, Carson had told some 50,000 Orangemen, 'With the help of God you and I joined together . . . will yet defeat the most nefarious conspiracy that has ever been hatched against a free people . . . We must be prepared . . . the morning Home Rule passes, ourselves to become responsible for the government of the Protestant provinces of Ulster.' This demonstration defined Ulster's policy and methods for the next three years. In January 1912, after first obtaining the sanction of the local magistrates, the Ulster leaders openly began to raise and train an army, the Ulster Volunteer Force, as a means of providing the provisional government with a force with which to resist Home Rule. Further support came on 28 September 1912, when almost half a million Ulster loyalists signed the Covenant, a semi-religious, semi-political document. The Volunteer army and the Covenant combined to form an effective means of disciplining Ulster supporters while providing a safety-valve for their emotions. General Sir George Richardson, a retired Indian Army officer, was appointed Commander-in-Chief of the Ulster Volunteers, whose recruitment, training, and arming proceeded apace. The illegal purchase and importation of arms was begun under the skilful direction of Captain Frederick Crawford, but it was not until the Larne incident in April 1914 that adequate supplies of arms and ammunition were obtained. Money was contributed by Ulster businessmen and gentry, and by Unionist sympathisers such as the 'British League for the support of Ulster and the Union'. By January 1914, over £1 million had been received by an indemnity guarantee fund to compensate members of the Ulster Volunteers for loss of life or disability. The Ulster Unionist Council, acting as a provisional government, directed these activities with amazing efficiency, appointing sub-committees to deal with the vital business of food and medical supplies, transport, and communications. Such preparations were not secret, and clearly foreshadowed rebellion against the British government, but Asquith preferred 'to let sleeping scorpions lie'.

Meanwhile, in England, the Unionist party was taking unconstitutional action to prevent the passage of the Home Rule Bill. Bonar Law and other leading Unionists were pressing George V to use his powers to veto the Bill and dissolve Parliament by dismissing his ministers. The Unionists were confident that they would win the general election. The King, while prepared to grant Home Rule to Ireland if that was what was wanted, was nevertheless conscious of the religious and political dangers that would result. He felt that 'whatever I do I shall offend half the population'. Taking advantage of the King's doubts, Bonar Law unscrupulously urged him to intervene in the Ulster crisis, with the result that George V passed on Unionist advice to Asquith together with his own pleas for a compromise on Home Rule. Asquith was frequently embarrassed by the King's persistence, but in September 1913, in a memorandum to the King, he firmly indicated what the constitutional position was regarding the use of the royal veto and the right to dismiss ministers. Asquith refused requests for a general election on the ground that it would settle nothing.

It was to please the King, however, that Asquith agreed to find a basis for compromise with the Unionist leaders, although he was sceptical about the outcome of such talks so long as the Unionists refused to accept the fundamental principle of Home Rule. Secret negotiations began in the autumn of 1913 between Asquith and Bonar Law, who met on three occasions at the home of Sir Max Aitken. Nothing was achieved; but a misunderstanding arose, for Bonar Law thought that his outline of an exclusion scheme for Ulster had been accepted by Asquith, and that Asquith would urge it upon the Cabinet. In fact, Asquith had merely been sounding out the possibilities for bargaining over Ulster, conscious as ever of the 'chasm of principle' between the two sides. Subsequent meetings with Carson were similarly fruitless. It was clear that the efforts of both Asquith and the

Unionist leaders were hampered by their supporters. Asquith was unwilling to make any concession that would weaken Redmond's standing with his followers, while Bonar Law, ever the loyal party man, did not want to run the risk of another 'Diehard' revolt by making concessions over Home Rule.

The situation in Ireland continued to deteriorate. Redmond had lost touch with the people in whose name he spoke, and the delay in achieving Home Rule had further weakened his position. The extremist policies of Sinn Fein spread. In October 1913, the strikers of the Dublin tramways had set up the Irish Citizen Army for their own defence. Led by James Larkin, a Socialist, and Captain J. R. White, an Ulster Protestant but a Nationalist, it preached a revolutionary form of socialism which helped to bring the Nationalist movement nearer to the use of force. In November 1913, the Irish Volunteers were formed by Professor John MacNeill, a Celtic archaeologist, and Patrick Pearse, a schoolmaster who taught Gaelic, to indoctrinate public opinion and to act in the nationalist cause should insurrection occur. The movement was set up neither to fight for Home Rule nor to fight the Ulster Volunteers. However, under the shadowy direction of the extremist Irish Republican Brotherhood, the Irish Volunteers appeared as a rival military force to that in Ulster. Redmond, a loyal Parliamentarian to the last, was embarrassed by the existence of the Irish Volunteers. The attitude of such extremists made it almost impossible for him to make concessions to Ulster at a time when Asquith was urging the need for concession.

Two private armies now faced each other in Ireland. The Government's problems were increased by well-founded rumours that the Unionists were threatening to use their majority in the House of Lords to amend the Annual Army Act, and thus prevent the Government from using the Army, its last resort, to enforce Home Rule in Ireland, until after a general election. That Bonar Law did not after all carry out his threat does not diminish astonishment that he could entertain a plan endangering the very basis of military discipline in Britain at a time of serious domestic and international crisis.

Thus, by the end of 1913, Asquith was forced seriously to con
sider the exclusion of Ulster from his Home Rule Bill. Cabinet
discussions, guided by Lloyd George, resulted in an Amending
Bill which proposed that any Ulster county might, by a vote of
its parliamentary electors, exclude itself from the operation of
the Home Rule Act for a period of six years, after which it would
automatically be brought in. The Bill was a tactical exercise,
designed to make it difficult for the Unionists to reject so reasonable a measure and to maintain their military organisation in
Ulster for a further six years. Redmond, having at first been unwilling to concede more than 'Home Rule within Home Rule' for
Ulster, reluctantly accepted the Government's proposals, which
were put before the Commons on 9 March 1914. Carson rejected
the Bill outright: 'We do not want sentence of death with a stay
of execution for six years.' The political atmosphere was electric.
It was widely believed that the Government was taking out war-
rants for the arrest of the Unionist leaders. The Government's
determination to move against Ulster seemed to be reflected in a
speech made by the First Lord of the Admiralty, Winston
Churchill, at Bradford on 14 March. Accusing the Ulster Provisional Government of being a 'self-elected body, composed of
persons who, to put it plainly, are engaged in a treasonable conspiracy', he concluded with an open challenge: 'Let us go forward together and put these grave matters to the proof.' At the
time of speaking Churchill knew that military and naval action
against Ulster had already been set in motion.

4 The Curragh Incident—towards civil war By March
1914, the Government had lost patience with Ulster and was fast
losing control of the situation. The final attempt to reach a constitutional settlement acceptable to all sides had come to nothing
when Carson rejected the conciliatory Amending Bill. A military
solution to the Ulster problem seemed the only alternative.
When, however, the Government attempted to use the Army to
reinforce its political position in Northern Ireland, an Army
Brigade refused to move and the Government backed down. This
episode, known either as the 'Curragh Mutiny' or the 'Curragh

Incident', is both controversial and illuminating, for it reveals not only the extent to which the politically neutral Army had become involved in the rights and wrongs of Ulster, but also the total ineptitude of the Liberal administration during the crisis. When the Army in Ireland proved unreliable, the Government could do nothing to prevent open rebellion.

The Army was clearly embarrassed over Ulster. Firing on one's fellow-countrymen is a most difficult assignment, for it offends the individual conscience and strains military discipline. Many officers and men were Ulstermen by birth and therefore sympathetic to Ulster's resistance. Senior officers actively helped the Ulster cause. The much revered Field Marshal Roberts, an Ulsterman, had recommended General Richardson as commander of the Ulster Volunteers. Another Ulsterman, General Sir Henry Wilson, held the important office of Director of Military Operations at the War Office. Through his ability and charm, Wilson had risen rapidly from Captain to Major-General, and to a post which gave him access to important military secrets. Wilson was a schemer, and worked in close collaboration with the Unionist leaders between 1913 and 1914. He felt no compunction about using his knowledge of the Government's intentions to further the interests of Ulster. Although Wilson had advised Bonar Law against amending the Annual Army Act, the Army had been unsettled by the rumours.

The Government would clearly have to handle the Army tactfully if and when it was used against Ulster. Their awareness of the possibility of officers resigning their commissions rather than fight in Ulster had led to a War Office conference on 16 December 1913 between the Secretary of State for War Colonel Seely, and his commanding officers. Unfortunately Seely, a rather arrogant man, had failed to soothe their anxieties about Ulster

By March 1914, only by using the British Army could Asquith hope to enforce his wishes in Northern Ireland. A small Cabinet sub-committee on Ulster had been formed, and on 12 March it sanctioned precautionary measures in Ulster. Churchill ordered the Third Battle Fleet to Lamlash in the Firth of Clyde, sixty miles from the Antrim coast, and two cruisers to Kingstown. On

14 March Colonel Seely warned General Sir Arthur Paget, the British C.-in-C. in Ireland, that, according to reports reaching the Government, attempts might be made in various parts of Ireland 'by evil-disposed persons' to raid Government stores of arms and ammunition, and that he was to reinforce these strategic points. Paget was made uneasy by these orders since Ulster was quiet at the time, and he feared that increased troop movements might cause unnecessary tension in the province. On 18 and 19 March he went to the War Office in London for talks to clarify the situation. He raised the possibility of officers resigning. Seely unwisely agreed that those officers with homes in Ulster could 'disappear', but that others who refused to carry out orders in Ulster should be dismissed. A brave but muddle-headed officer, Paget misunderstood his instructions (which, surprisingly, had not been put in writing) and, on returning to Dublin on Friday 20 March, he made the situation worse. Calling his senior officers together, he excitedly described the Government's precautions against Ulster as an act of war, and, instead of giving orders for the maintenance of law and order in the province which would most probably have been obeyed, he gave them an intolerable choice. His tone was rude and bullying; those officers unwilling to cooperate against Ulster were threatened with resignation and dismissal from the service. That evening, General Sir Hubert Gough, an Ulsterman by birth and upbringing but not domiciled in the province, reported to Paget that he and fifty-seven officers of the Cavalry Brigade, stationed at the Curragh, would resign their commissions rather than serve in Ulster. Further resignations were imminent. This could be called a mutiny, and the Army's actions made the Government's position critical, for it could no longer depend on the full support of the Army. In Ulster, the Volunteers, well briefed on Government intentions by General Wilson, had mobilised, and Carson and the Unionist M.P.s had returned from Westminster to lead them. The Government's troop movements, reinforced by the Navy, were in operation. However, on learning the news from the Curragh at Friday midnight, Asquith was forced to abandon the possibility of a military solution to the Ulster crisis.

The political repercussions of the 'Curragh Incident' were no less damaging to the Government. On 21 March Asquith, who had allowed his impetuous colleagues Churchill and Seely too much freedom of action, claimed that it had all been a misunderstanding. Cancelling the fleet movements and issuing placatory statements to the King and to the Press, he appeared to have the crisis well under control. Gough and the Colonels were ordered to report to the War Office, where on the Monday they met Seely, Field Marshal Sir John French, the C.I.G.S., and General Sir Spencer Ewart, the Adjutant-General. Gough was determined not to return to Ulster without a written guarantee that the Army would not be used in hostile operations in Ulster. Taking full advantage of his opponents' weakness, Gough returned to Ireland in triumph, bearing a Cabinet Note, altered without prior Cabinet approval first by Seely and then by French, which stated that the Army would not be called on 'to enforce the present Home Rule Bill on Ulster'.

The whole affair from start to finish had been mismanaged by the Government. A political storm raged for the next month. Asquith faced a barrage of criticism from friend and foe alike. Although he publicly repudiated the unauthorised alterations to the Cabinet Note, he preferred to do nothing further about Generals Wilson and Gough, who got away with their disloyalty, much to the disgust of many M.P.s. Seely, French and Ewart resigned; Asquith himself took over the War Office. Details of the precautionary measures which the Government had taken in Ulster were published in two White Papers, but the Unionists, thoroughly informed by Wilson on the exact measures taken by the Government, ruthlessly pressed home the charge that there had been a plot to coerce Ulster.

No definitive evidence has ever been published to confirm or deny such a plot, although strong circumstantial evidence seems to substantiate its existence. There is little doubt that, on the surface, Ulster was calm in March 1914, with no sign of a preemptive strike by the Ulster Volunteers against Government arsenals, even though plans for such an eventuality had been prepared by the Ulster provisional government. Asquith continued to allege that he had got his information about the 'evil-disposed persons' from police reports; at no time, however, were any further details of such persons published. The Ulster operations sanctioned by the Cabinet sub-committee were, moreover, on a far greater scale than the mere safeguarding of arms depots against the Ulster Volunteers. Too many important questions, such as the failure to give Paget precise orders, remained unanswered and reinforced the impression that the Government must still have something to hide. Unionist fury was concentrated on Churchill. He was already hated for his apostasy to the cause which his father had so nobly espoused. His truculent speech at Bradford and the fleet movements he had ordered had been a major part of the Government's attempt to intensify the pressure on Ulster. Bonar Law had put down a vote of censure on the Government for 28 April, but news of the Larne gun-running diverted attention from the Government's obvious embarrassment.

On the night of 24/25 April over 25,000 rifles and 3,000,000 rounds of ammunition (historians cannot agree over the exact numbers) were landed for the Ulster Volunteers at Larne, Bangor, and Donaghadee. It was a brilliant coup, well-planned and perfectly carried out. The efficiency of the Ulster Unionist organisation contrasted sharply with the incompetence of the Government's representatives in Ireland, who learnt of the gun-running only after the arms had arrived and had been dispersed throughout the province. Ulster was now armed. It was this grim fact which convinced Asquith that a compromise must be found before violence erupted between the Ulster Volunteers and the Irish Volunteers.

Private negotiations reopened in the summer between Asquith, Bonar Law, Carson and Redmond on the terms for the exclusion of Ulster, but the differences between the two sides were as irreconcilable as ever. Redmond would allow exclusion only within a strict time limit, while Carson wanted exclusion with no time limit. No agreement could be reached on the exact area of Ulster to be excluded. Certain 'Diehard' Unionists were still opposed to the very thought of Home Rule. It was, however, agreed that the changes to the Home Rule Bill would be included in a separate Amending Bill which would receive the Royal Assent on the same day as the Home Rule Bill. On 25 May 1914, the Home Rule Bill passed the Commons for the third and last time. On 23 June, the Government's Amending Bill, repeating the offer of 9 March, was introduced into the Lords, where it was completely altered by extreme Unionist amendments—all the nine counties of Ulster, including the overwhelmingly Catholic and Nationalist areas such as Donegal, were to be excluded without plebiscites and without a time limit. Although it was obvious that these amendments would be totally unacceptable to the majority in the Commons, the Bill would have to be passed within the next month, since by this time the Home Rule Bill would be ready for the Royal Assent.

Total deadlock had been reached, and Asquith agreed to the King's suggestion of an all-party Conference, which met at Buckingham Palace from 21 to 24 July. The Unionists only attended out of deference to the King's wishes, while Asquith was equally pessimistic about the talks. Not surprisingly, the Conference was a total failure. No agreement was reached on the vital question of areas to be excluded, and the equally important question of the time limit was not even discussed. On 26 July, the Irish Volunteers attempted a daylight landing of rifles at Howth, near Dublin. They found their way back to Dublin barred by British troops. A scuffle developed, but the Volunteers got away with their rifles. The troops were jeered at and stoned when they returned to Dublin. As they marched along Bachelor's Walk shots were fired; three people were killed and thirty-eight wounded. The Nationalists immediately accused the Government of favouritism in allowing Ulster's gun-running to go unpunished, while punishing them. The events at Bachelor's Walk further undermined Redmond's tenuous hold over his people. Asquith's Irish policy was bankrupt: war in Ireland seemed inevitable.

As it happened, civil war in Ireland was averted by events of even greater significance on the continent of Europe. The Austrian ultimatum to Serbia had set in motion a chain reaction which was to lead to war between the Great Powers. On 30 July, while Asquith was still searching for a solution to the Irish question, Bonar Law and Carson asked to meet him. They requested the postponement of the Home Rule and Amending Bills in order not to advertise Britain's internal dissensions. On 4 August Redmond, who in the previous June had established his leadership over the Irish Volunteers, generously agreed to cooperate with the Government. However, on 18 September 1914, the Home Rule Bill became law, together with a Bill to suspend its operation until the end of the European war in which Britain was now engaged.

In their handling of the Irish Question in these years the Liberals had committed many cardinal errors. Having first imposed an undemocratic solution which was intolerable to the people of Ulster, they then expected the Protestant minority in Ireland to behave in the best traditions of British liberalism by passively accepting the decisions of the majority. They appeared to be applying British remedies to an Irish problem. Ireland has had no opportunity for the democratic traditions of peaceful change to grow—of minimal violence, of the minority accepting the decisions of the majority and of the majority not taking decisions which the minority regards as genuinely intolerable. Her bloodstained past has scarred her to this day. Bitter racial and religious conflict, fear and suspicion made the Protestant people of Ulster unwilling to accept the rule of their hated enemies, the Catholics in the South. It was the Liberals' tragedy that they had failed to appraise the true nature of Ulster's misgivings; that their mismanagement had made the situation there more impossible; and that a democratic solution to the Ulster problem was now out of the question.

Chapter VI

Liberal England 1911-14

1 The 'death' of Liberal England   The Liberals, having achieved so much in their period of office between 1905 and 1911, seemed to lose their momentum in the years immediately preceding the outbreak of war. The Government simultaneously faced three important domestic crises. While Asquith and his lieutenants struggled to find a solution to the Irish problem, they also had to deal with labour unrest on an unprecedented scale and with violent outrages committed by militant women in support of their claim to the vote. The Liberals often appeared helpless either to satisfy or to restrain the demands made upon them. Their failure has provoked a major debate between historians. G. D. H. Cole, Raymond Postgate and George Dangerfield among others share the belief that the years 1910-14 witnessed the death of Liberal England. Cole and Postgate allege that 'the great Liberal experiment, begun so glamorously with the electoral victory of 1906, was ending in ignominious rout'.

However, Henry Pelling, Trevor Wilson, and Samuel Beer have presented the alternative thesis that, although the Liberal party had its troubles, it was generally in good health on the eve of war. In fact, Dr. Wilson says, 'The outbreak of the First World War initiated a process of disintegration in the Liberal party which by 1918 had reduced it to ruins.' Only a close study of the Liberal Government's record between 1910 and 1914 can determine which of these two interpretations is the more valid. G. D. H. Cole and Raymond Postgate, two distinguished Socialist

118

historians, maintain that Liberalism, the all-powerful economic and political ethos of Victorian Britain, had become moribund as a result of the new economic, social and political forces that had arisen by the first decade of the twentieth century. The fundamental Liberal belief in individualism, best served by free trade and minimal state intervention, was being superseded by collectivism and the belief that the individual's interests would best be protected by increased state help. Liberals had believed in government by persuasion, in representative parliamentary democracy, where the majority would respect minority interests and the minority would accept the will of the majority. Interparty consensus underpinned the political system and provided a means of compromising differences. Cole and Postgate advance the thesis that between 1910 and 1914, 'more and more evidently, the Government was ceasing to govern, and parliamentary institutions were falling into disrepute. The spirit of revolt was spreading from one section of the people to another, and manifesting itself in a demand for new leadership and a new philosophy of life.' They support their argument by showing how the events of 1910-14 revealed inadequacies in the Liberal Party—notably the failure to make concessions, which provoked violent reactions from several powerful groups. The Unionists were in an ugly and unconstitutional mood following the defeat of the Lords in 1911. Abandoning the inter-party consensus, they were prepared to stop at nothing to defeat the Government. In supporting Ulster, they were willing to resist Home Rule with force and to exploit the Liberals' inability to devise a Bill that would satisfy the conflicting interests of North and South. The Liberal Government looked on helplessly as Ireland slid into a state of civil war that was averted only by a greater catastrophe in Europe. They go on to describe how the working classes turned against Liberalism. Aware that capitalist profits were rising and their own incomes were falling, the workers had looked to the Government for redress. The Liberals, however, being too closely identified with the capitalist interest and unwilling to tamper with the existing social and economic system, had said that the workers' demands could not be afforded at a time of increasing world competition for trade. As a result, working men, disillusioned with traditional parliamentary methods, turned to 'direct action', to militant trade unionism and syndicalism, and consequently British industry was paralysed by strikes. Furthermore, the Liberals' failure to grant demands for a limited form of female franchise had led the militant suffragettes, contemptuous of unsuccessful constitutional efforts in the past, to a form of civil disobedience more violent than anything that had gone before. The Liberal Government, according to Cole and Postgate, 'could not see its way to resisting the demands except by force, and it was well aware of the danger that, if it resorted to force against force, it might speedily cease to be Liberalism, and forfeit its claim to govern'.

In his highly contentious work, *The Strange Death of Liberal England*, George Dangerfield embroiders this theme of Liberal downfall even more extravagantly. 'The story of these years', he says, 'deserves to be told, if only for the spectacle it affords us of a democracy passing from introspection to what looks very like a nervous breakdown.' His book, he asserts, 'is not a record of personalities but of events; and not of great events but of little ones, which, working with the pointless industry of termites, slowly undermined England's parliamentary structure until, but for the providential intervention of a world war, it would certainly have collapsed . . . It was in these years that that highly moral, that generous, that dyspeptic, that utterly indefinable organism known as the Liberal party died the death. It died from poison administered by its Conservative foes, and from disillusion over the inefficacy of the word "Reform". And the last breath which fluttered in this historical flesh was extinguished by War.' He claims that 'by 1910 the ideal of personal security through respectability had become putrid: therefore it was necessary that it should die'; the rejection of Victorian security and respectability by the Unionists, workers, and women between 1910 and 1914 'was a brief but complete phase in the spiritual life of the nation'. The Liberal leaders, he alleges, were undemocratic and 'airy, remote and irresponsible', possessed with 'the spirits of whimsy which only afflicts Englishmen in their weakness'.

Elie Halévy, the great French historian, is among those who interpret the period 1910-14 as a time of 'domestic anarchy'. He traces a common pattern of violence in the agitation of Unionists, Irish, workers and suffragettes. He sees Liberalism failing to satisfy the grievances of the workers and being replaced by socialism. It is his contention that the workers, having 'a growing distrust and contempt for politics', turned to extreme forms of socialism, more particularly the new syndicalist doctrines, and it is to the influence of the latter that he attributes the industrial unrest of the pre-war years.

Professor Glaser, a prominent historian of English Noncon- formity, has contributed to this theme of Liberal disintegration by pointing to the correlation between the decline in Noncon- formity and the collapse in the political fortunes of Liberalism. He argues that the close spiritual and material links between the Nonconformist conscience and Liberalism had greatly nurtured the Liberal Party during the nineteenth century, forming what W. E. Gladstone had called 'the backbone of British Liberalism'. 'In the broadest sense', Glaser maintains, 'the Nonconformist conscience embraced the whole of the Nonconformist political outlook . . . Both Nonconformity and Radicalism found their strength in the commercial and industrial centers of provincial England. In these flourishing cities the leading members of the Nonconformist chapels were the local captains of industry, the spearheads of municipal reform, and the magnates of the local Liberal party.' By 1914, he asserts, Nonconformity, weakened by political divisions over Home Rule, imperialism, and socialism, and becoming ever more limited to the prosperous middle class, was losing touch with the real issues and interests of large sections of the new democracy. It is his conclusion that: 'The ebbing of the Nonconformist conscience entailed the gradual loss of the Liberal party's practical political strength, and more important, the loss of the religious ethos and moral passion which had distinguished English Liberalism in its creative golden age.'

Seeing the Liberals' demise as the inevitable outcome of the 'forces of history', Marxist historians have not hesitated to join the debate over their downfall. They have argued that the

Liberals' extension of the franchise to the working classes in 1867 and 1884 had unleashed political and economic forces that fostered the rise of socialism. In defeating the House of Lords, they destroyed the last serious barrier to democracy and completed their historic mission. The emancipated working class, anxious to transform the political system to harmonise with its own economic interests, refused to accept a party which was both 'herald of [political] emancipation and nurse of capitalism'. Keith Hutchison, a Marxist writer, draws the conclusion: 'Now that emancipation had acquired a socialist connotation, these two functions were openly in conflict and, as a consequence, the Liberal Party began to disintegrate, with some of its members pulled to the right and others to the left. Even if the First World War had not produced a fatal schism among the Liberals, it is doubtful whether they could have long remained a major force.'

Historians of the Cole-Dangerfield tradition thus raise fundamental questions as to the competence of the Liberal Government in the pre-war period. Was the Government's apparent failure due to the errors of the party, to the eclipse of Liberal values, or simply to bad leadership? The Liberals' mistaken response to the conflicting demands of Irish Nationalists and Ulstermen has been discussed in a previous chapter, and their ineffectiveness as Ireland drifted inexorably towards civil war is generally accepted. It would appear that, as both Liberal principles and the Liberal leaders were to a large extent responsible for the Irish tragedy, the Cole-Dangerfield thesis is substantiated on this particular point. When, however, the argument is examined that labour unrest signalled a rejection of Liberal values by the working classes and an increase in socialism and syndicalism, doubts begin to arise.

2 Industrial unrest   The Railway Servants' Union's call for a national rail strike in 1907, in support of a wage rise and recognition of the railway unions by the employers, heralded a new era of labour militancy on an unparalleled scale. The Government, fearful of the possible effects on the economy of a national rail strike, intervened and prevented its taking place. Thanks to

Lloyd George's successful mediation from the Board of Trade, a compromise acceptable to both sides was reached; conciliation boards were set up for each railway, and although the companies were not required to recognise the unions, they would meet the workers' representatives on the boards to discuss wages and hours. It was improvised forms of negotiation and settlement such as these that opened a new chapter in British industrial relations.

Nevertheless, because of a general slump in trade, more time was lost through industrial stoppages in 1908 than in any of the previous ten years. Exports declined, while unemployment rose. The shipbuilding employers in the north-east, faced with empty order books, resorted to wage cuts, the usual practice when sales fell. A four-month strike was followed by an employers' lock-out. Elsewhere in the north-east, the Amalgamated Engineers, against the advice of their leaders, came out in a seven-month strike against wage cuts. Churchill, now at the Board of Trade, helped to get the men back to work. Although compelled to accept the wage reductions, they were promised independent conciliation boards for the future.

In 1909-10 came trouble in the mines. The Government's Eight Hours Act (1908) had disappointed the miners. Everywhere traditional working habits were disrupted and home life disturbed when, in 1909, the Act came into operation. Strikes followed in Yorkshire, South Wales, Northumberland and Durham. Late in 1910, the miners of Ely Colliery at Tonypandy in South Wales refused to accept new wage rates offered for opening a new coal seam and were locked out. Five pits, also owned by the Cambrian combine, struck in sympathy. The strike, noted for its rioting and the subsequent police and troop movements that were sanctioned by the Home Secretary, Churchill, lasted until August 1911, when the men returned to work on terms they could have had before they struck. It was successive strikes and lock-outs of this type that poisoned relations between men and management.

There were strikes among Southampton seamen and dockers in 1911, and unrest spread quickly to transport workers in other ports, causing rioting, looting and bloodshed. When G. R. Askwith, the Government's industrial 'trouble-shooter', went to Hull he 'heard a town councillor remark that he had been in Paris during the commune and had never seen anything like this: . . . he had not known there were such people in Hull— women with hair streaming and half nude, reeling through the streets, smashing and destroying'. Troops were used in many places and rioters killed in Liverpool and Llanelly. Once again there was the threat of a national rail strike, and although Asquith appreciated the men's grievances, when he intervened to stop the strike he only made things worse. His threat that he would not hesitate to 'employ all the forces of the Crown' merely increased the men's determination to strike. Lloyd George saved the day. By stressing the dangers of the international situation and by finding a peace formula, he got the men back to work. It appears, however, that the quite unusual degree of violence that accompanied the industrial disputes in 1911 was due to the practice of employing blackleg labour, protected by troops and police, in the docks, railways and mines, and to the blazing hot summer that year which brought tempers to the surface.

The wave of militancy continued into 1912, when the greatest number of days lost by stoppages in any pre-war year was recorded. The miners demanded a national minimum wage—the 'five and two' as they called it, or five shillings per shift for men and two shillings for boys. Having failed to persuade the owners to meet their claims, the whole Miners' Federation had gone on strike in February. Two million men were laid off and British industry was disrupted. When the Government belatedly intervened, its efforts to find an acceptable settlement were fruitless. Finally, accepting the principle of the minimum wage, the Government rushed the Minimum Wages Bill (Coal) through all its stages in March 1912. The men reluctantly returned to work in April; they had not got what they wanted even though the important principle of the minimum wage had become law. When the lightermen, dockers, and carters in the London docks struck because they refused to work with non-union labour, they were reduced to complete surrender by the refusal of the

Port of London Authority to give way. This was the last major pre-war industrial dispute, although labour unrest continued in 1913-14 with a series of small strikes in the Midlands and the long struggle between the tramway employers and the Irish Transport Workers Union in Dublin. Bitter industrial strife prevailed until the outbreak of war.

What had caused the unrest? It would appear that the fundamental reasons were economic. The cost of living had risen by some four or five per cent between 1902 and 1908, and by a further eight points between 1909 and 1913. The rise in money wages had kept pace between 1902 and 1908, but had lagged behind between 1909 and 1913. Thus the pressure on trade unions to seek wage increases was correspondingly greater. Moreover, the rise in the cost of living did not hit all the workers in the same way. Those who were better off were better able to survive a fall in the relative value of wages than the manual worker, for whose labour there was no steady demand and whose wages therefore rose and fell more irregularly. This would explain why industrial unrest in the years 1906-14 was largely confined to two sectors: unskilled and lower-paid labour on the one hand, and on the other, workers in two industries, coal-mining and railways, who were prepared to coerce their employers by industrial action.

The cases of the railwaymen and miners illustrate the plight of the lower-paid workers particularly effectively. Railwaymen's wages had been falling behind those of other wage-earners since the 1880s. Hours of work were long and career prospects poor. The Act of 1894, regulating goods rates in perpetuity, had restricted profits at a time when prices were rising. Just as the companies were trying to cut costs by means of wage reductions, the men were demanding wage rises that would enable them to keep pace with other wage-earners. Similar problems beset the coal-mining industry. Falling productivity since the late 1880s and steadily rising costs (caused, for example, by the implementation of the Eight Hours Act) were not offset by any increased demand for coal. The mine-owners had reacted with wage cuts and a stricter interpretation of the rate paid for the various kinds of coal seam. Overall, the miners' wages were falling, creating bad labour relations and demands for strikes.

A marked increase in the power of trade unions had coincided with the men's demands for more militant action. The Trade Disputes Act (1906), passed in response to Labour pressures, had reversed the Taff Vale decision and restored the rights enjoyed by trade unions under the Acts of 1871 and 1875. Picketing, sympathetic strikes, and secondary boycotts were henceforth within the law, while a union could not be sued for damages unless the action complained of had been committed with the sanction of the union executive.

A further factor working in favour of the unions was the second wave of 'new unionism': union membership, especially among seamen, dockers and general labourers, rose by over sixty per cent between 1910 and 1914. Pelling explains this rise in union membership in terms of the exceptionally low unemployment rate in the years 1911 to 1914, and draws the conclusion, 'Men could more readily defy their employers when the supply of potential blacklegs was at its lowest.' The workers' bargaining position was further strengthened by the joining together of unions to form such amalgamations as the National Transport Workers' Federation in 1910 and the National Union of Railwaymen in 1913.

It seems clear, moreover, that a substantial number of workers were becoming disillusioned with the traditional channels for improvement, and that there was an ever-widening gulf between the older generation of conservative union leaders and the rank and file, many of them young, articulate and convinced that their leaders had 'sold out' to the very system they were trying to change. Indeed, leading trade unionists like Richard Bell had been given lucrative employment by the Government. A number of union leaders remained Liberal in their political sympathies while the Labour M.P.s had conspicuously failed to break out of the Liberals' shadow and devise a political programme they could call their own. Parliament often appeared to be conspiring against the interests of the working-class electorate. The Government never consulted working men about what they wanted or did not want in the the way of social reform. According to Pelling, 'The progressive legislation of the period was in great measure sponsored by middle-class reformers, partly for humanitarian reasons, partly because they thought that social reform would be electorally popular.' In reality, the working classes were more worried about rising prices and unemployment. While they welcomed non-contributory old age pensions, they resented strongly having to pay the national insurance contributions in 1912, and some of the labour unrest could be attributed to this.

The Osborne Judgement (1909) and the Government's four years' delay in reversing this highly provocative legal decision made matters worse. A Liberal trade unionist, W. V. Osborne, Secretary of the Walthamstow Branch of the Railway Servants, decided to bring an action against his union for contributing a compulsory levy from the members' subscriptions to the funds of the Labour Party. He claimed that such expenditure was *ultra vires* for a trade union. He lost his case in the High Court, but the Court of Appeal reversed the decision, and was unanimously confirmed in its action by the Law Lords, who granted him an injunction to prevent his union from raising a political levy and from making a contribution to Labour Party funds. Their verdict had profound consequences. Labour M.P.s, deprived of their main source of income, were made even more dependent on the Liberal Party to secure redress. The T.U.C. was outraged and determined to press for immediate legislation to reverse the Law Lords' decision. When the Government, preoccupied on many fronts, seemed to be dragging its feet, a minority of trade unionists turned away from the constitutional processes of Parliament and the law.

Cole and Postgate, and Halévy have contended that the workers now took to 'direct action' for revolutionary political purposes, as advocated by the syndicalists, and that consequently industry was crippled by strikes. The syndicalist movement in Britain drew inspiration from the ideas of the American Marxist, Daniel De Leon and of the Frenchman, Georges Sorel. The essence of this revolutionary creed was the conviction that the workers, by using their industrial power rather than parliamentary methods, could win control over the industries in which they worked. This would lead to the introduction of a new organisation of society. Tom Mann, the leader of the 1889 strike, had become acquainted with syndicalist ideas in France, and had returned to Britain determined to inject them into the political and industrial system. In 1910, therefore, he launched the Industrial Syndicalist Education League. A number of Left-wing groups (the Socialist Labour Party, the Central Labour College, the Plebs League) and the South Wales Miners' Federation were inspired by syndicalist dogma, but it is clear that only a small minority of trade unionists were fully committed. While it is true that syndicalists played an active part in forming the Transport Workers' Federation in 1910, their call for a national strike in support of the London dockers in 1912 evoked little response, while the Dublin Transport Workers' strike, led by the syndicalist, Jim Larkin, was regarded with deep suspicion by the majority of British trade union leaders. The syndicalists had only limited success in their attempts to bring about workers' control through the closer co-operation of unions in industry. The amalgamation of three out of five railway unions in 1913 was as much the result of long-standing rank-and-file discontent, for example with the 1907 conciliation boards, as of syndicalist pressure. Syndicalist efforts to reorganise unions such as the miners, the engineers, and the builders' labourers all failed. The formation of the 'Triple Alliance' in 1914, whereby the transport workers, railwaymen and miners agreed to terminate their contracts simultaneously, might appear to accord with the syndicalist belief in a general strike 'to put an end to the Capitalist system'. In fact, the decision to co-operate more closely was principally inspired by the damage done to unionists in other industries by a national strike in a single industry. The railway unions, for example, had had to pay over £100,000 in unemployment benefits to its members laid off during the 1912 coal strike. Moreover, the majority of union leaders involved in the 'Triple Alliance' saw its main purpose as strengthening their bargaining position in order to secure higher wages and better conditions for their members, and to control militancy rather than engineer a social revolution. Indeed, as

G. A. Philipps has written, 'The "general strike of 1914" is, it seems, a mirage of historians treading the infertile deserts of British labour history in search of a *révolution manquée.*' In the light of this evidence, it is difficult to sustain Halévy's view that the labour unrest was primarily a 'Syndicalist Revolt'.

The vast majority of trade unionists throughout the period 1910-14 continued to put their faith in the traditional methods of advancing their interests. The high turn-out in the two 1910 elections (the 86.6 per cent figure in January was the highest in any twentieth-century British general election), the steady rise in the number of Labour constituency parties, and the increase in trade union applications for affiliation to the Labour Party would appear to contradict any claim that the working class as a whole was rejecting representative democracy. The Parliamentary Committee of the T.U.C. and the Parliamentary Labour Party, reinforced by the miners' M.P.s' decision to become Labour instead of Liberal, formed two influential pressure groups at Westminster. The Liberal Government may indeed have been tardy in reversing unpopular anti-union decisions in the courts, but the fact that they did eventually pass the Trade Disputes Act of 1906 and the Trade Union Act of 1913 is clear evidence that they could not ignore the demands of the representatives of the working classes in Parliament.

The charge that the Liberal Government were responsible for the workers' protest and that they aggravated relations between Capital and Labour remains to be examined. While it is true that their belief in the social and economic status quo ruled out any fundamental changes in the organisation of industry, they undoubtedly made a positive effort to understand, to help, and to satisfy trade union grievances wherever possible. It is difficult to fault the mediation in industrial crises of Lloyd George and Churchill and of Sir George Askwith, their highly competent conciliator. The Government went on to create permanent machinery for disputes (conciliation boards, the use of arbitration and the Industrial Council), and frequently appeared to side with the workers in the battle with their employers. Moreover, by carrying out important industrial reforms, such as the Eight

Hours Act, the Trade Boards Act, and the Minimum Wages (Coal) Act, they achieved real progress for working men that was not always appreciated by them at the time. Thus, it is hard to believe that in its handling of the 'labour question' either the Liberal Government or the Liberal approach was in process of 'nervous breakdown'.

3 'Votes for women' Whereas the Liberals may be acquitted of Dangerfield's accusation of being 'airy, remote and irresponsible' in regard to their handling of industrial unrest, it is difficult not to apply his graphic description to their treatment of women's demands for enfranchisement. John Stuart Mill had begun the parliamentary campaign for women's suffrage as far back as 1867, when he tried unsuccessfully to amend the Reform Act so that it would include female as well as male householders. The respectable, constitutional movements for women's suffrage set up after 1867 by Miss Becker and Mrs. Fawcett had continued to present a reasoned case for women's suffrage and to create a decisive shift of public opinion in favour of a moderate measure of reform. However, their attempts to persuade Parliament failed, and failure produced disillusionment and contempt for the constitutional approach among a militant female minority who, by their fanaticism and increasingly anarchical activities, posed a severe challenge to established authority.

Women had attained a wide measure of social and political emancipation in the latter part of the nineteenth century. They enjoyed greater domestic freedom, more social rights under the Married Women's Property Acts, wider opportunities in education, entry to many professions, and the right to participate in local affairs. They sat on School Boards and as Poor Law Guardians, and some had even gained the vote in local elections under the Municipal Corporations Act (1869) and the Local Government Act (1894). It seemed logical that women should have the vote in parliamentary elections. As *The Times*, a redoubtable opponent of female suffrage, was forced to admit: 'The admission of women to the municipal franchise itself affords an apparent presumption in favour of their admission to the electoral franchise.' (Quoted by W. L. Arnstein, 'Votes for Women: Myth and Reality', *History Today*, August, 1968.) However, innate prejudice and political difficulties barred the constitutional way to votes for women. Frederick Pethick-Lawrence, who played a very important part in organising the suffragette movement, has summarised the anti-suffragist case as follows: 'Men, it was said, were governed by reason, women by emotion. If once the franchise were thrown open to women, they would speedily obtain a majority control and force an emotional policy on the country to the detriment of the public weal. In particular it was said (though less openly) that on sex matters women were narrower and harder than men; and that if they were given power they would impose impossibly strict standards of morality, and endeavour to enforce them by penalties for non-observance. A further fear was that, if women came to share the political, intellectual, and occupational life of men they would lose their special charm and attraction. A slightly different motive was the innate love of domination. This was sometimes expressed in the blunt rejoinder: "Votes for Women, indeed: we shall be asked next to give votes to our horses and dogs." ' Prejudice was not confined to men alone. Queen Victoria summed up the conventional belief in what was fit and proper: 'The Queen is most anxious to enlist everyone who can speak or write to join in checking this mad, wicked folly of "Women's Rights", with all its attendant horrors, on which her poor feeble sex is bent, forgetting every sense of womanly feeling and propriety. Lady – – – – – ought to get a GOOD WHIPPING.'

Frustrated by the failure of constitutionalist efforts to obtain women's suffrage, Emmeline Pankhurst and her daughters, Christabel and Sylvia, had formed the Women's Social and Political Union, known as the 'suffragettes', as opposed to the 'suffragists', as members of the constitutional societies were called. Their objective was 'immediate enfranchisement'. Mrs. Pankhurst added, 'We shall work not by means of any outworn missionary methods but by political action.' They began a policy of all-out attack on the newly-elected Liberal Government in 1906, promising them that there would be no peace until their demands were met. The first act of militancy occurred in 1905 when Christabel Pankhurst and Annie Kenney interrupted one of Churchill's election meetings. Forcibly removed from the hall, they were subsequently arrested for disturbing the peace outside. Christabel, refusing to pay a fine of ten shillings, opted to spend a week in jail. The incident gained more publicity for the cause of women's suffrage than a whole year of peaceful agitation could have done. Militant tactics were increased. Public demonstrations, processions to Parliament, a policy of 'Keep the Liberal out' in by-elections, and the physical harassment of prominent Liberals frequently led to skirmishes with the police, arrests, and unduly severe punishments in the courts. Miss Theresa Billington, for example, was fined ten pounds with two months' imprisonment in default of payment for ringing the door-bell of Asquith's house! The tactic of the prison hunger-strike was begun in 1908, and when the Government retaliated with 'forcible feeding' to keep the prisoners alive the militants were able to invest the cause of women's suffrage with the halo of martyrdom. This campaign of militancy was initially successful, bringing publicity for the movement and friendly co-operation from the suffragists, whose less dramatic but no less important efforts to obtain votes for women continued until 1914. Above all, the suffragettes managed to goad Parliament into taking the question of female suffrage seriously.

The suffragettes had suspended their militancy during 1910-11 when an all-party Conciliation Committee was trying to find a women's suffrage Bill that would satisfy the newly-elected Commons, but its failure led to a revival of suffragette militancy on an unprecedentedly hysterical and violent scale in 1912-14. The women henceforth deliberately flouted the law. A policy of secret arson was begun. Pillar-boxes, country houses, churches, a school and a railway station were set on fire, and property was attacked. Acid was poured on golf-courses, paintings in art galleries were slashed, and every plate-glass window in Regent Street was broken. On Derby Day, 1913, a suffragette, Emily Davison, threw herself under the King's horse and was killed. When arrested, the suffragettes continued their agitation with hunger-strikes in prison. Its patience exhausted, the Government introduced the 'Cat and Mouse' Act (1913) which enabled the Home Secretary to release any prisoner whose health was suffering, and to rearrest her on recovery. Without such methods, concluded Reginald McKenna, the Home Secretary, 'thirty or forty would come forward to die. They are fanatical and hysterical women, who no more fear death in fighting what they believe to be the cause of women than the natives of the Soudan feared death when fighting the battle of the Mahdi.' What had provoked certain Englishwomen to reject the rule of law and the parliamentary process and to resort to fanatical outrages? How far was the Liberal Government responsible? The answers to these questions may help to determine whether, as its critics allege, 'Liberalism had reached an impasse' and 'the Liberal party died the death'.

The political objections to female suffrage were an even greater obstacle than male prejudice. When in power, neither the Liberals nor the Unionists were prepared to make women's suffrage a government question. Successive Liberal leaders, Gladstone, Campbell-Bannerman and Asquith, were afraid that as only well-to-do single women would be enfranchised under a household suffrage (the existing qualification for men), they would be drawn by their age and possessions to vote Unionist, and that the 'balance of parties would be upset'. Although the majority of Liberal backbenchers were friendly to the cause, they could do little while their leaders were so hostile. The Unionist position presented an almost direct contrast. Whereas Disraeli, Northcote, Salisbury, Balfour and Bonar Law were in favour, Unionist backbenchers were uniformly hostile. Thus, it was left to private members to introduce female suffrage, but without tacit government approval and sufficient parliamentary time, their Bills were all too easily 'talked out' and lost. This was the fate of the 1908 and 1909 Private Members' Bills. It was little wonder that women began to rebel against the traditional methods of obtaining their place within the constitution.

Above all, it would appear that the procrastination of Asquith's ministry was responsible both for discrediting constitutional

methods and for causing the suffragettes to turn to civil disobedience. The Prime Minister was actively hostile to the idea of
extending the franchise to women. As he told the Commons
during the debates on the 1912 Conciliation Bill, 'I oppose this
. . . on the broad and simple grounds that in my opinion, as a
student of history and of our own public life, experience shows
that the natural distinction of sex, which admittedly differentiates
the functions of men and women in many departments of human
activity, ought to continue to be recognised as it always has been
recognised, in the sphere of parliamentary representation.'
Taking advantage of the real political barriers to women's suffrage,
the limited amount of parliamentary time available (the People's
Budget, the Parliament Bill, social reform and Home Rule were
all before Parliament at the same time as women's suffrage) and
the growing volume of anti-suffrage opinion, Asquith deferred
action, thereby provoking the suffragettes. Mrs. Fawcett summed
up his importance: 'Opposition from a Liberal, with all the
Liberal traditions of devotion to the principal of representative
government and a wide suffrage, was far more damaging to our
cause than opposition from Conservatives.'

   While Asquith and other important Liberals may have delayed
votes for women, others—Lloyd George, Churchill, Haldane,
Grey—were in favour, and it was this pro-suffrage lobby in the
Cabinet that instigated increased Government action from 1910
onwards. An all-party Conciliation Committee produced a Bill
granting the vote to every woman who had the necessary household or ten-pound occupation qualification. It passed its second
reading in July 1910, by 299 votes to 189, but the large minority
against it convinced the Government that it could not give further
facilities to the Bill, which was therefore dropped. Conciliation
Bills in 1911 and 1912 were no more successful. In June 1912,
Asquith introduced a major reform measure, the Franchise and
Registration Bill, designed to destroy plural voting and property
qualifications for voting. It was the Government's intention that
the Bill should be amended to include female suffrage. It passed
its second reading, but when the debate on the committee stage
opened in January 1913, Mr. Speaker Lowther ruled in answer to

a question that, since amendments granting women's suffrage would change the nature of the Bill, it would have to be withdrawn and a new Bill introduced. Asquith therefore promised time for women's suffrage in a private member's Bill, but this measure was defeated by forty-seven votes in May, 1913, and women had still not got the vote when the First World War broke out.

Although the Speaker's ruling on the 1913 Franchise Bill was not the Government's fault, Asquith revealed his true feelings when he wrote privately to Venetia Stanley: 'The Speaker's coup d'état has bowled over the Women for this session—a great relief.' Moreover, there seems to have been an unfortunate disparity between the timid way the Government handled practically open rebellion in Ireland and their inhumane use of forcible feeding and the 'Cat and Mouse' Act when dealing with militant women. Dr. Rover spotlights the failure of the Liberals and indeed of Liberalism on this issue: 'As women were required to prove they wanted the vote without being able to ballot on the subject, they could only have recourse to demonstrations and agitation. If they behaved in an orderly manner, they were told that they did not show sufficiently strongly that they demanded enfranchisement and that they were weak, dependent creatures who ought not to have it. If on the contrary, they resorted to violence it was said that their behaviour proved they were unfitted to exercise the vote. Indeed an impasse!'

It is impossible, however, to condemn the Liberals entirely for what happened, since the suffragettes' unwillingness to compromise and their unscrupulous campaign of violence were ultimately self-defeating. As early as October, 1908, Arthur Ponsonby, a Liberal supporter of female suffrage, was writing to Lady Constance Lytton, 'I think that militant tactics were effective up to a point. They have got beyond that point . . . they have got the House of Commons for the time being dead against them and are rapidly alienating opinion in the Country.' In their fury, the suffragettes mistakenly concentrated their attacks on the Liberals, who, in spite of the inaction of their leaders, were the women's best hope of success since they were on balance the party more sympathetic to them. Politically damaged by suffragette activities, particularly in by-elections, the Liberals were even less disposed to meet their demands. Moreover, as Professor Arnstein has observed, 'The law-minded Prime Minister, understandably enough, was not attracted to a cause whose adherents vilified him, broke the windows of his home, threw a hatchet at him, and sought to tear off his clothes.' One must therefore agree with the conclusion of Dr. David Butler: 'If the militant suffragettes had not overreached themselves, some measure of female suffrage would probably have been achieved, but their violence exacerbated fears of what women might do with the vote if it were granted.' (*The Electoral System in Britain since* 1918, O.U.P., 1963.)

4 Epilogue   The basic thesis of the Cole-Dangerfield school and of the Marxists, that Liberalism and the Liberal party were so far advanced in the throes of death by 1914 that their replacement by Socialism and the Labour party was inevitable, remains to be examined. If a Government's achievements are a reliable criterion, then it is difficult to reconcile the Liberals' massive successes (the foundation of the modern Welfare State, the victory over the Unionists and the House of Lords, and far-reaching measures of army and navy reform) with the charge that 'the Government was ceasing to govern'. Furthermore, it seems highly unlikely that a party containing within its ranks in 1914 such formidable political talents as those of Lloyd George, Churchill and Asquith could be 'dying'. In truth, there was no serious rival to Liberalism in 1914. Conservatism, in the form of the Unionist Party, was at a low ebb. Frustrated by their lack of success since 1900, Unionist leaders accepted representative democracy only so long as they controlled it, yet they had no alternative to it. Socialism and syndicalism still had relatively few followers. Politically, the Liberal party was dominant on the Left. In August 1914, they held 261 seats in the Commons to Labour's 36, convincing evidence that Labour's electoral challenge had not made any significant impact before 1914. In fact, Labour candidates had done badly in the 1910 general elections and in by-elections since. Professor Beer notes of Labour in 1914 that 'the bulk of the party, in short, shared a general frame of thought and values within which it carried on its politics of interest, and this perspective could still be fitted into the ideology of Liberal Radicalism'. He concludes, 'So long as Labour's purposes were simply those of trade union politics, framed in the broad terms of Radical ideology, the independence of the party was still seriously in doubt. Indeed, there remained the real possibility that it might become simply a wing of a more socialistic, though not Socialist, Liberal Party.' (Quoted in J. A. Thompson, *The Collapse of the British Liberal Party*.) The Liberals, moreover, were taking the initiative in proposing and carrying out the great political, social and defence reforms of the pre-war period. Lord Dalton, a leading Labour Cabinet Minister, has recalled: 'The Liberals, indeed, were making the running in those years.' Could this be the party 'whose day was definitely done'?

It must be admitted, however, that the omens for Liberalism were not entirely favourable. The party leaders were exhausted in 1911-14 after carrying out their legislative programme, and were seriously at fault in their treatment of the Irish Question and Women's Suffrage. There were signs that twentieth-century Liberalism was failing to cope with new political, economic and social forces, in contrast with the success of Gladstonian Liberalism only a few decades before. The old link with the working classes was being eroded. Co-operation between English Liberalism and Celtic Nationalism in Wales, Scotland and Ireland was drawing to an end. As Nonconformity declined (and there is little evidence to contradict Professor Glaser's view that it did), its appeal was more to the middle than the working classes. Too few local Liberal Associations were prepared to sponsor working-class candidates, who, as a result, looked to the Labour party and trade unions for their entry into Parliament. Increasingly British society and politics were being divided on class lines, and Liberals, unwilling to change the existing social and economic structure, found themselves all too often being identified with capitalist interests. For example, when industrial disputes embittered relations in the South Wales coalfield, the miners looked to Labour to redress their grievances, as most of the mine-owners were Liberals. By 1914, the Liberal party had not resolved the fundamental conflict between its wealthy 'individualist' Right and its radical and moderately 'collectivist' Left. Here lay Labour's future opportunity. While it is true that the Labour party was not supplanting the Liberals at the polls before 1914, there was nevertheless a steady growth of Labour organisation at constituency level, and, according to Pelling, 'Among the workers . . . a sort of undogmatic "Labourism" was establishing itself, which consisted in little more than the opinion that the Labour Party, and not the Liberals, was the party for working men to belong to.'

The parallels and connections that Professor Halévy saw between the Irish, feminist and labour revolts would appear to be no more than 'an accidental convergence of unrelated events'. The years from 1910 to 1914 constituted a turbulent period in domestic politics, constantly overshadowed by international tensions. The Liberal Government was being forced on to the defensive by circumstances beyond its control, and, if Liberalism and the Liberal Party were doomed, it was as a result of long-term social and economic factors that made their greatest impact on British politics only after the cataclysmic effects of the First World War.

Chapter VII

Preparations for war

1 Reform of the Army While in opposition, the Liberal Party had been deeply divided by questions of foreign policy and defence. The New Liberals, who continued the 'Little England' and the Radical tradition, wanted peace, which they felt would best be ensured by steering clear of military alliances and diplomatic commitments, and by 'retrenchment' in arms expenditure. The Liberal Imperialists, on the other hand, recognised that Britain's international position was now threatened by the steady deterioration in Anglo-German relations, particularly by the development by Germany of a rival fleet. The Liberal Imperialists had supported the Unionist Government in its policies of diplomatic alignment with Japan and France and reform of the armed forces. Germany had taken advantage of Russia's defeat in her war with Japan (1904-5) to test the Anglo-French Entente, but German tactics in the Moroccan crisis (1905-6) had only succeeded in driving the two powers closer together. As G. P. Gooch pointed out, 'The contingency of joint resistance to a common foe had been envisaged for the first time.' Unofficial military talks were held between the French and British general staffs in December 1905 and January 1906 and, according to Professor Marder, informal naval talks may have taken place earlier. By 1906, it was apparent that the European storm centre had passed from the Mediterranean to the North Sea.

The Liberals had taken office during the Moroccan crisis. Although the old Radical, Campbell-Bannerman, had become

Prime Minister, he had nevertheless promised that policy would remain unchanged in foreign affairs and defence. The key appointments in these fields were given to Liberal Imperialists; Sir Edward Grey succeeded to the Foreign Office, and Richard Burdon Haldane to the War Office. Lord Tweedmouth went to the Admiralty, where the real authority lay with the First Sea Lord, Admiral Sir John Fisher. Campbell-Bannerman, Grey, Haldane and Fisher realised that two highly significant factors had emerged by the winter of 1905-6: Britain, although she was not bound by any formal alliance, would support France if she was attacked by Germany, and, whatever the cost, the German naval challenge would have to be met. The Liberal ministers and their professional advisers alone knew and accepted the precise nature of Britian's commitments and needs, for circumstances dictated that such information should be kept secret from the rest of the Cabinet, from Parliament, and from the people until the last possible moment. Grey assessed the British position exactly: 'If the German Fleet ever becomes superior to ours, the German Army can conquer this country. There is no corresponding risk of this kind to Germany: for however superior our Fleet was, no Naval victory would bring us any nearer to Berlin.' The Royal Navy, then, had to prepare for a war with Germany that Englishmen more and more regarded as inevitable. Fisher revealed his thoughts on the subject in a letter to King Edward: 'That we have eventually to fight Germany is just as sure as anything human can be, solely because she can't expand commercially without it.' Grey was acutely aware of the military implications of the diplomatic policy he was pursuing towards France and Germany. However, as Anthony Morris has written, 'For more than half a century it had been accepted military policy that the primary function of the British Army was the garrisoning of the Empire and the protection of its land frontiers.' (Haldane's Army Reforms, 1906-8: The Deception of the Radicals, *History*, February, 1971.) The Boer War had revealed conspicuous deficiencies in the military machine—the Army's movements had been ponderous, its weapons and tactics out of date, and its staff work poor. Thus it was imperative that the British Army be reformed and an expeditionary force prepared for rapid dispatch to France, Britain's new friend, in the event of a German attack on her.

The Unionists had been only moderately successful in their attempts to reform the army. Balfour had founded the Committee of Imperial Defence in 1903 to place the strategic and military needs of the Empire under surveillance, thus creating an effective mechanism for planning defence. In 1903-4, the Esher Commission had investigated the working of the War Office and the Government had accepted its report. Successive War Ministers, St. John Brodrick and Arnold-Forster, consequently introduced measures that improved the 'brain-power' and administration of the British Army. A general staff was set up within the War Office, while the Army Council was appointed as a single collective body to decide policy and supervise administration, personnel and armament. War Office administration was rationalised. But far-reaching proposals to produce an ever-ready expeditionary force and an effective reserve came to nothing. The Army was virtually unchanged, a state of affairs which led Lord Roberts, a much-respected former Commander-in-Chief, to complain to the House of Lords in July 1905: 'I have no hesitation in stating that our armed forces, as a body, are as absolutely unfitted and unprepared for war as they were in 1899-1900.'

Such was the problem Haldane inherited on his appointment to the War Office, where he was to remain until 1912. In that period he rebuilt the Army from top to bottom. His achievement was primarily due to the personal qualities he brought to the task. Endowed with a first-class intellect and much political skill, he was anxious to apply to the Army the most recent developments in technology, education and management. At the same time he was prepared to listen to his professional advisers at the War Office, where Minister and advisers soon worked as a team. Facing his task without preconceived ideas on military reform and willing to learn from his predecessors' failures, Haldane spent 1906 in close examination of the Esher Report. His lucid mind enabled him to grasp what had to be done: 'We had therefore to provide for an Expeditionary Force which we reckoned at six great (i.e. with three instead of two brigades) divisions, fully equipped, and at least one cavalry division. We had also to make certain that this force could be mobilised and sent to the place where it might be required as rapidly as any German force could be.' (Quoted by Corelli Barnett.) But Haldane always had to proceed with great caution. The military conversations with France and Belgium were so secret that the true purpose of the army reforms had to be disguised. This was not easy. Moreover, Haldane had many enemies. Campbell-Bannerman disliked him and had expected him to fail at the War Office, the graveyard of so many political reputations. Many New Liberals questioned the sincerity of his Liberalism. It was alleged that expediency rather than principle governed his actions. They drew comfort from the Prime Minister's election speeches supporting peace, and confidently expected economies in the defence estimates and a greater concentration on social reform. Haldane was faced with determined scrutiny from their representatives in the Cabinet, Lloyd George, Winston Churchill and Lewis Harcourt, who were ever watchful against increased spending on arms.

Haldane handled these problems with consummate skill. Relying on the powerful support of King Edward, his fellow Liberal Imperialists, the War Office generals and influential figures like Lord Esher and Colonel Repington, Defence Correspondent of *The Times*, he was able to get round his critics by single-minded determination and the skilful use of guile. He was all things to all men, confusing his critics by a studied vagueness so that the true significance of his proposals was disguised. He indicated that the purpose of the Expeditionary Force was to maintain the defence of the Empire and spoke of 'Indian garrisons' and of an 'Imperial police force'. He dealt with objections that his reforms might lead to the imposition of conscription by stressing the voluntary nature of some of his proposals, for example, the territorial scheme, and he met the desire for 'retrenchment' by effecting considerable economies in the Army estimates. These fell from £29,810,000 in 1905 to £28,840,000 in 1914, even though prices in general had risen by eighteen per cent in that same period. So that Britain could better defend herself, he was quite prepared to play off the New Liberals' demands for economies against the Unionists' calls for increased spending, and thus diverted attention from what he was really up to. In the final analysis, he confounded his critics by his complete mastery of military policy.

Haldane set about his task of reform with certain basic principles in mind—the Army's role must be a subordinate one, confined to dealing with emergencies; the forces based in the United Kingdom must be able to provide in a continental war an expeditionary force ready to be shipped abroad in the shortest possible time; the reserves should be reorganised and prepared for war if required; and all this must be done economically. His first step was to reorganise the home field army and reserves. When he had enquired in 1906 how many men would be available to form an expeditionary force from a total Army strength of some 650,000 troops, he was told 80,000 at the end of two months. His plan was to raise the British Expeditionary Force (the B.E.F.) from the Regular forces stationed in Britain and from a reorganisation of the Reserve strength. His Army Order on 1 January 1907 put his reforms into motion. He found a supply of troops for a six-division B.E.F. from a more concentrated use of existing manpower. The below-strength third regimental battalions were disbanded, while the remaining two battalions were brought up to full strength. The B.E.F. would be raised from those battalions stationed in the United Kingdom. A seventh division could be speedily formed from troops in relatively near foreign stations and from surplus troops at home. Britain at last possessed a highly professional and efficient Field Force which could be immediately mobilised on the outbreak of war.

The reform of the Reserve began with the Army Act of 1907, which abolished many archaic units such as the militia, the yeomanry and the volunteers. Special new reserve units were created, bearing the old militia regimental titles in order to safeguard recruitment. Reservists would enlist for six years, spend six months in training, and attend a fortnight's camp annually. The formation of this Territorial Army, as the force was called, was perhaps the most spectacular of Haldane's achievements. Supported behind the scenes by the King, he was able to pass his Territorial and Reserve Forces Bill through Parliament in 1907 and have it accepted by the local magnates, who had been offended by his treatment of the militia. The scheme came into operation on 1 April 1908. The new force was drawn from the recently disbanded yeomanry and volunteers, and would be liable for service anywhere in the United Kingdom, but not abroad. It would consist of fourteen infantry divisions and fourteen mounted brigades organised in the same way as in the regular army, equipped with its own artillery and transport, and run by 'County Associations', which, as a gesture to the local landed interests, were under the control of the Lords Lieutenant. The Reserve Force was an immediate success. By the beginning of 1910 it was up to 88 per cent of its establishment, numbering 276,618 officers and men. The real significance of Haldane's organisation of the B.E.F. and his reform of the Reserves is best appreciated in the light of what happened when war came. Some twenty divisions of British troops (six regular and fourteen territorial) were mobilised punctually and without difficulty in August 1914; a few weeks later, very heavy casualties in the Field Army were replaced by adequate Reserves.

The preparation and efficiency of the B.E.F. were further assisted by wide-ranging reforms in the superstructure of the Army. The general staff system was introduced throughout the Army, while the creation of Officers Training Corps in universities and public schools provided valuable military experience and attracted significant numbers of candidates for commissions. A new Army textbook, Field Service Regulations, was introduced, and the Army was retrained in tactics, staff work and administration. Haldane was anxious to reduce the time needed for mobilisation and movement to the theatre of war, and a committee of railway managers was appointed to control the rail traffic of mobilisation. A 'War Book' was compiled by a subcommittee of the Committee of Imperial Defence which laid down every action to be taken on mobilisation by every ministry and branch. It proved of enormous value in August 1914.

Haldane had almost completed his reform of the Army when he left the War Office in 1912. Professor Cyril Falls, while praising the simplicity and ingenuity of Haldane's reforms, is nevertheless critical of certain aspects of his work. Faced with constant political pressure to reduce the Army Estimates, Haldane responded with economies which often led to serious deficiencies in equipment. The Army was kept short of the guns and ammunition it required, as well as of such vital equipment as motor ambulance wagons, mobile kitchens and telephones. Its fighting efficiency was undoubtedly impaired by excessive parsimony. On the other hand, Morris considers that 'Haldane had achieved his object. He had laid the foundations for the best possible Army that time and circumstances allowed . . . He had provided Grey with the necessary forces to implement the entente should that eventuality arise'. The B.E.F. gallantly withstood the stern test of circumstances in 1914. In the light of this evidence, it would appear that Haldane justly deserves his reputation as one of the greatest Secretaries of State for War in Britain's history.

2 Reform of the Navy The Royal Navy provided the British Isles' main line of defence. Not since Trafalgar had Britain's naval supremacy been contested. The Navy's impressive numerical strength had bred self-satisfaction and resistance to change. The result was an inefficient Navy, run on out-dated traditions, strategy and tactics, with old-fashioned ships and weapons. The passage of the German Navy Acts, designed to ensure that 'if the strongest naval power engaged it (the German Navy), it would endanger its own supremacy', came as a rude awakening and a challenge. The Royal Navy responded under the inspired leadership of Admiral Sir John Fisher and a naval revolution followed. Owing nothing to high birth, wealth or influence, 'Jacky' Fisher had reached the top through his own genius. Fisher was successively C.-in-C. Mediterranean, Second Sea Lord, C.-in-C. Portsmouth, and First Sea Lord (October 1904 to January 1910). He was a human tornado who, with vision, enthusiasm, administrative pertinacity, and indefatigable determination revitalised the Edwardian Navy. 'Economy and efficiency', declares

Professor Marder, 'were the motives underlying Fisher's great reforms. Like Napoleon, he was that very rare bird, the fighting man who considers the taxpayer.' Naval estimates had risen sharply from £23,778,400 in 1898-99 to £36,889,000 in 1904-5. Convinced that lavish expenditure reduced efficiency, Fisher agreed with those politicians who urged economies in defence spending.

Fisher shared the Admiralty's concern at the German naval threat. Lord Selborne, the First Lord of the Admiralty, had distributed a Memorandum to his colleagues in Lord Salisbury's Cabinet in November 1901 which stated, 'The more the composition of the new German fleet is examined, the clearer it becomes that it is designed for a possible conflict with the British fleet.' This fear of the German Navy was to be a determining factor in the policies of every British Government up to the outbreak of war. Furthermore, as a result of the diplomatic rapprochement which brought Britain on to the side of France a policy of concentrating Britain's naval forces in home waters was initiated in December 1904. An Admiralty Memorandum in 1906 explained, 'Our only potential foe now being Germany, the common-sense conclusion is that outlying Fleets no longer require to be maintained at the strength which was admittedly necessary a year ago when France and Russia were our most probable opponents.' Fisher believed war with Germany was inevitable, and his overriding aim was to make the Fleet both efficient and ready for that war when it should come.

Confident that the end justified the means and convinced that the reforms must be accomplished within his five-year term of office, Fisher was drastic in the methods he employed. He was prepared to stop at nothing in pushing through those reforms he thought essential for the Navy's efficiency. An unscrupulous reliance on favouritism and a vindictive treatment of opponents, personal indiscretion and increasing megalomania made him a highly controversial figure. A much-publicised quarrel between Fisher and Admiral Sir Charles Beresford, the leading defender of those archaic traditions that Fisher was sweeping away, had divided the Navy into distinct pro- and anti-Fisher factions and had produced widespread ill-feeling. As Churchill remarked, 'The "Band of Brothers" tradition which Nelson handed down was for the time, but only for the time, discarded.'

Fisher's innovations began between 1899 and 1904. The 'Selborne scheme' brought important changes in the recruitment and training of officers and cadets and improved their esprit de corps, while at the same time pay, prospects and living conditions for the Lower Deck were improved and discipline made less brutal. Higher morale was the result. The Fisher Revolution began in earnest with his appointment as First Sea Lord in 1904. Having previously promoted his supporters to those positions where they could be of use to him and having worked out his proposals to reshape the Navy in complete secrecy, Fisher simultaneously implemented four major and interdependent reforms. In order to improve the efficiency of the Reserve Fleet so that it almost equalled the fleet in commission, he entirely reorganised it. Under the existing system, ships in the reserve were divided into those ready for mobilisation but not immediately required and those under heavy repair and out of commission. Fisher resented this inefficient and expensive use of manpower and money. Consequently sixty ancient warships in the Dockyard Reserve were scrapped, and skilled personnel redirected to the 'nucleus-crew' system which he had introduced. The warships of the Reserve Fleet would henceforth be manned by two-fifths of their normal crews and would exercise regularly. The importance of the 'nucleus crew' system and the reform of the reserve fleet was that it achieved a more economical use of manpower and kept the whole fleet as ready for war as was consistent with peace-time requirements. Further trained personnel for the new reserve were found through a ruthless scrapping of obsolete warships. Scores of British vessels were scattered over the globe, 'showing the flag' or engaged in unimportant police duties. These 'Snail' and 'Tortoise' classes, as Fisher described them, 'could fight no modern warship larger than themselves, even when they could fight at all, and their speed was insufficient to enable them to run away'. Fisher therefore struck 154 ships off the effective list, dividing them into 90 'sheep' (condemned as useless), 37 'llamas' (assigned to minor duties) and 27 'goats' (laid up without crews). By this measure alone, Fisher saved valuable berthing space, money and manpower.

The redistribution of the Fleet in December 1904 was the logical conclusion of these reforms. With Germany now regarded as the potential opponent of the Royal Navy, rather than Japan, France, Russia or the United States, Fisher saw that he must reorganise the strategic deployment of British fleets and squadrons. They would henceforth be concentrated in the North Sea and Channel, rather than in the Mediterranean, for, as Admiral Jameson rightly points out, 'If the Fleet in home waters was defeated in battle the war would be lost. Setbacks abroad would be inconvenient, but not a major disaster.' (*The Fleet that Jack Built*, Hart-Davis, 1962.) The foreign squadrons were reorganised first. The Cape Squadron was responsible for the North American. South Atlantic, and West African stations, while the Eastern Fleet, based at Singapore, was to control the oceans east of Suez. They would be reinforced in peace-time by independent squadrons of armoured cruisers. The Mediterranean Fleet was reduced from twelve to eight battleships, while the old Channel Fleet, renamed the Atlantic Fleet, based at Gibraltar with eight of the latest battleships, was to reinforce when required either the Mediterranean Fleet or the new Channel Fleet. The latter was a force of sixteen battleships, created out of the old Home Fleet and based at Dover, forming by 1904-5 the most powerful British fleet. The fleets were to exercise regularly in home waters and would be strengthened in wartime by squadrons of armoured cruisers. Further naval dispositions in the North Sea followed between 1906 and 1909, when all the naval forces in home waters were united in the Home Fleet. The significance of Fisher's redistribution lay in the fact that a powerful fleet of the best and fastest ships was now concentrated in the North Sea—that is, on the probable battleground with the potential enemy, Germany.

Fisher's originality can be seen in his contribution to naval construction. He had kept up to date with technological, strategic and tactical developments, and wished to introduce the latest innovations in armaments, gunnery, speed, mobility, power and design into the new Navy he was creating. He believed that battleships, armoured cruisers, destroyers and submarines must have priority in naval building, and he set up a committee at the Admiralty, packed with his supporters and with the foremost experts, to design the new vessels. However, the idea for the 'Dreadnought' came from the Italian ship-designer Colonel Cuniberti, who proposed an ideal battleship with a uniform main armament of ten twelve-inch guns, stout armour protection, and a minimum speed of twenty-one knots produced by turbine engines. The first of the new 'Dreadnought' class big ships was completed in record time between October 1905 and December 1906. Fisher's second major technical innovation was the armoured or 'battle' cruisers of the 'Invincible' class. He had envisaged that, with a speed of twenty-five and a half knots and an armament of eight twelve-inch guns, their primary role would be to scout and to destroy enemy commerce-raiders; if necessary, they could act as a fast wing in a fleet action to reinforce the van or the rear of the battle fleet. The introduction of the Dreadnought programme aroused a storm of controversy at the time. Fisher's critics believed that it was his greatest blunder, objecting to it on technical, strategic and political grounds. It was argued that fighting power and protection had been sacrificed in order to gain superior speed and that the six-inch gun should not have been eliminated in favour of the all-big-gun armament. By deliberately nullifying Britain's battleship predominance and encouraging other nations to get on more even terms, Fisher, it was claimed, had ushered in a new era of naval competition with Germany, which would entail increased spending on armaments that would soon eat up the considerable economies he had achieved in naval costs. However, modern historians of the Royal Navy have been generous in their praise of Fisher's revolutionary warships. Captain Peter Kemp writes, 'At one stroke every other battleship in the world was outdated and Britain had gained a lead in ship design, if not yet in ship numbers, that would enable her to keep ahead in sea power.'

Political objections to the increased naval expenditure entailed by competition with Germany were a further obstacle. The new

Liberal Government, elected to some extent on the promise of retrenchment in armaments expenditure, was seriously embarrassed by the naval arms race. The deep-rooted contradictions in Liberal foreign and defence policies were thrown into sharp relief when the party took office, and from 1905 to 1914 the government was driven to constant and uneasy compromise between Liberal principles and the pressure of circumstances. For the defence ministers, national security rather than economies was the first concern. Thus the successive Liberal First Lords of the Admiralty, Lord Tweedmouth, McKenna and Churchill, all accepted the counsel of their professional advisers, Fisher in particular, and advocated a 'big Navy' as the best defence against Germany, even if this meant increasing naval estimates and postponing social reform. For his part, Fisher was prepared to meet the Government's wish for economy wherever possible. The New Liberals, however, believed that the money needed for social reform, to which they were pledged, could never be secured unless 'bloated armaments' were checked. Backed by *The Nation* and *The Manchester Guardian*, they argued that a Liberal Government should work for peace and set an example by cutting arms spending. They pointed to 'Fisher's proud claim of the Navy's omnipotence: if they could all sleep sound in their beds, then now was the time to switch some of the nation's wealth from battleships to slums'. They were 'little Navy' men and did not relax their pressure for economies in defence spending until war had broken out in 1914. An additional hazard was the popular interest in naval affairs, often fanned by a partisan press. For fear of antagonising Germany, the Government could not, for example, reveal the real reasons for controversial measures such as the redistribution of the Home Fleet. Ministers were forced to suffer in silence the uninformed criticisms of Unionist politicians and press, eager to gain political advantage by attacking the Government's handling of defence.

Campbell-Bannerman had accepted 'without prejudice' the Cawdor Memorandum of the outgoing Unionist ministry, which had enunciated future shipbuilding policy—four big ships a year. Lord Tweedmouth, First Lord until 1908, knew little about naval matters and was content to allow Fisher to pursue his programme. His successor, McKenna, was a first-class administrator who worked closely and successfully with Fisher until the latter's retirement from the Admiralty in 1910. Nevertheless, the Government made genuine efforts to appease its vociferous critics. Naval estimates had been £36,889,500 when Fisher was appointed First Sea Lord in 1904; by 1907-8 he had cut them to £31,419,500. Thereafter, increased Anglo-German naval rivalry and the adoption of the principle that Britain should have a sixty per cent preponderance over Germany in dreadnoughts and battle cruisers raised estimates to £51,550,000 for 1914-15. Liberal proposals for a halt to the naval arms race between Britain and Germany, during which heavy ships were removed from the British building programme between 1906 and 1908, failed, since Germany was determined to increase her relative strength. Britain's attempts to slow down the race in naval armaments at The Hague Peace Conferences from 1906 to 1907 were similarly unsuccessful. The clash of interests between the 'big Navy' and 'little Navy' lobbies came to a head in the 'Navy Scare' of 1909, which resulted in Asquith's compromise that four dreadnoughts would be laid down in 1909-10 and four more, if the necessity for them was proven, not later than 1 April 1910. When it was discovered that Austria and Italy were about to build dreadnoughts, the Government decided to lay down all eight at once 'without prejudice' to the 1910-11 programme. Continuing demands for naval economies were refused by a Government that was determined to maintain its lead over Germany in capital ships.

Winston Churchill had been a leading critic of naval expenditure until his appointment as First Lord of the Admiralty in 1911. His period of office illustrates the change that came over Liberal politicians once they were fully aware of the precise nature of Britain's defence commitments. The Agadir crisis of 1911 convinced Churchill of Germany's warlike intentions, and, with Fisher's help, he was determined to press on with the preparation of the Royal Navy for the coming war. He rapidly acquainted himself with every aspect of the Navy's work, and through his foresight and energy, achieved remarkable progress in the Navy up to the outbreak of war. He was adamant that the Navy must take advantage of the latest developments in matériel, even if it meant a drastic rise in estimates. The result was that the naval programmes between 1912 and 1914 were, in Churchill's words, 'the greatest additions in power and cost ever made to the Royal Navy'. He was prepared to take the responsibility for this upon himself and to use his powers of argument to wear down opposition to rising naval expenditure both in the Cabinet and in Parliament. On Fisher's prompting, he decided in 1912 to build a new fast division of battleships, the 'Queen Elizabeth' class, armed with fifteen-inch guns. To obtain the required speed of twenty-five knots, he took the vital decision to change the Navy from coal- to oil-fired engines, and the Anglo-Persian Oil Company was acquired by the Government to secure adequate supplies. Churchill's personal interest in the possibilities of air warfare led to the foundation of the Royal Naval Air Service, while the submarine arm, long one of Fisher's pet ideas, was expanded. Churchill prepared for all the eventualities of a German attack. In 1912 he set up a Naval War Staff, thus remedying a deficiency which had been the ostensible reason for Fisher's resignation in 1910. War games were played at the Admiralty, and the Navy practised its role in the event of invasion, blockade, combined operations, attacks on commerce, and fleet actions. Lieutenant-Commander J. M. Kenworthy made this estimate of Churchill's work at the Admiralty: 'This sea service in the years prior to the outbreak of hostilities was one long preparation for war. We expected war, we were ready for it, and almost wished for it.'

The new German Navy Law of 1912, aiming to achieve a 2:3 ratio in capital ships with Britain, and the failure of the Haldane Mission to Berlin to secure agreement over shipbuilding had renewed British fears. Anglo-German Naval rivalry was intensified. In 1912 a redistribution of British fleets essential to the security of the United Kingdom took place, which involved a weakening of Britain's Mediterranean position. As Fisher pointed out, '*We cannot have everything or be strong everywhere*. It is futile to be strong in the subsidiary theatre of war and not over-whelmingly supreme in the decisive theatre.' The Government's policy raised widespread misgivings. While the Unionists attacked the 'abandonment' of the Mediterranean and urged an alliance with France, most Liberals were horrified at the prospect of a French alliance—'an absurdly disproportionate remedy', *The Manchester Guardian* called it. Although naval and political commitment was dreaded by the Government, events dictated closer Anglo-French naval co-operation. In September 1912 the French concentrated their whole battle fleet in the Mediterranean, guarding their vital maritime communications with North Africa. French Channel and Atlantic coasts were left exposed to attack, but the French anticipated that the British would fill the void. After lengthy secret discussions, Anglo-French naval agreement was reached by February 1913. In theory the British Govern-ment was left with its hands free of any formal military alliance with France, but it was recognised that Britain would have a moral obligation to aid France in the event of a German attack on French ports on the Channel and Atlantic. Churchill sup-ported this arrangement, since he wished to ensure greater effic-iency should Britain decide to enter a war in which France was involved, and this was what the deployment achieved.

In October 1913, Churchill had suggested that, as an economy measure, a test mobilisation of the Third Fleet be substituted for the usual summer manœuvres in 1914. It was accomplished in July in only two days and was followed by a grand review of the fleet at Spithead. 'It constituted', boasted Churchill, 'incompar-ably the greatest assemblage of naval power ever witnessed in the history of the world.' The ships were about to disperse when, on 26 July, hearing that Serbia's reply to the Austrian ultimatum over the Sarajevo incident had been rejected, Prince Louis of Battenberg, the First Sea Lord, stopped the demobilisation of the fleet. On the 28th the Navy was placed on a 'preparatory and precautionary basis', and on 29–30, the fleet passed swiftly and under cover of darkness to its battle stations at Scapa Flow. With its lead in capital ships over Germany established, it was, as Professor Marder says, 'ready for all contingencies: the sallying forth of the High Seas Fleet, the attempted invasion of the United Kingdom, or an attempt to interfere with the transport of the B.E.F. or with Britain's oceanic trade'. At 11 p.m. on 4 August the Admiralty gave the order to 'commence hostilities against Germany'.

Although the immediate achievement of preparation and mobilisation in 1914 was Churchill's, it would appear that the major credit for a modern navy, ready to meet the German challenge, belonged to Fisher. Professor Marder believes he was a great man, and describes his period as First Sea Lord as 'the most memorable and the most profitable in the modern history of the Royal Navy . . . In the teeth of ultra-conservative traditions, he revolutionised the Navy, cramming into a few years the reforms of generations and laying foundations that can never be destroyed'. Many naval men, however, regarded him as a menace. His technical innovations were criticised for being inefficient and inferior. However, the untried nature of so many of his reforms of matériel and the urgency with which they were introduced meant that their limitations were not fully appreciated until put to the test of war. This was hardly Fisher's fault. His insistence on speed and superior heavy guns had led to lighter armour protection on British ships; some of the British losses at Jutland in 1916 can be attributed to this calculated risk. It is clear that in some fields (armour, mines, shells, torpedoes) the German Navy was superior, while the creation of adequate East coast naval bases and of good anti-submarine precautions was neglected. A further failing was Fisher's contempt for the Army—'a bullet fired by the Navy'; he opposed the dispatch of a B.E.F. to France, and would not co-operate with the Army in formulating joint war plans. This lack of understanding was to cost Britain dear during the war, for example, in the Gallipoli Campaign. Another great weakness was his opposition to any attempt to set up a naval staff to draw up war plans. He preferred to keep war plans to himself. He wrote, 'A Naval War Staff is a very excellent organisation for cutting out and arranging foreign newspaper clippings . . . so far as the Navy is concerned, the tendency of these "thinking establishments" on shore is to convert splendid sea officers into very indifferent clerks.' It was not surprising that when a Naval War Staff was set up in 1912, it did not have long enough to establish itself before the outbreak of war. Finally, Fisher's violent and uncompromising methods had shattered the unity of the Navy, and only the common dangers of war with Germany healed the wounds he had inflicted on the service. Nevertheless, Fisher must be judged by his achievements. Winston Churchill wrote, 'His great reforms sustained the power of the Royal Navy at the most critical period in its history', while Captain Peter Kemp has made this balanced assessment: 'Fisher's reforming zeal, his vision, and his ruthless energy left behind him a navy so revitalized and so alive to change that it could face the coming war with confidence. During those years of power he *was* the navy, and it was his work which had laid so surely the foundations of the British victory at sea which in 1918 brought the German empire down to ruin.'

Further Reading

General

S. Nowell-Smith (ed.), *Edwardian England* (O.U.P., 1964)—contains several authoritative and readable chapters. R. C. K. Ensor, *England 1870–1914* (O.U.P., 1936)—the standard work, good on political issues but dated. E. Halévy, *History of the English People in the Nineteenth Century, Epilogue, Part I, Imperialism and the Rise of Labour, 1895–1905,* and *Part II, The Rule of Democracy, 1905–1914* (Benn, 1961)—the classic narrative account. G. D. H. Cole and R. Postgate, *The Common People 1746–1946* (Methuen, 1938)—lively and informative. G. Dangerfield, *The Strange Death of Liberal England* (Paladin, 1970)—controversial and stimulating. C. Cross, *The Liberals in Power 1905–14* (Pall Mall, 1963)— a good general account. H. Pelling, *Popular Politics and Society in Late Victorian Britain* (Macmillan, 1968)—some brilliant essays. I. Jennings, *Party Politics Volumes 1–3* (C.U.P., 1960–3)—a stimulating political analysis.

Biographies

R. Jenkins, *Asquith* (Collins, 1964)—essential reading. K. Young, *Arthur James Balfour* (Bell, 1963)—useful. R. Blake, *The Unknown Prime Minister, Andrew Bonar Law* (Eyre and Spottiswoode, 1955)—a masterly work. P. Fraser, *Joseph Chamberlain* (Cassells, 1966)—interesting. R. Rhodes James, *Churchill. A Study in Failure 1900–1939* (Weidenfeld and Nicolson, 1970)—a penetrating re-examination. R. Churchill, *Winston Churchill. Volume II, The Young Statesman 1901–1914* (Heinemann, 1967)—a mine of information. P. Magnus, *Edward VII* (John Murray, 1964)—first class. H. Nicolson, *George V* (J. Constable, 1952)—excellent. C. L. Mowat, *Lloyd George* (Clarendon, 1964)—adequate. M. Thomson, *David Lloyd George* (Hutchinson, 1948)—satisfactory. N. H. Brasher, *Arguments in History* (Macmillan, 1968)—contains useful biography of Chamberlain. J. W. Derry, *The Radical Tradition* (Macmillan, 1967)— has good biography of Lloyd George.

Party Histories

R. Blake, *The Conservative Party from Peel to Churchill* (Eyre and Spottiswoode, 1970)—an excellent analysis. R. B. McCallum, *The Liberal Party from Grey to Asquith* (Gollancz, 1963)—useful. A. Bullock and M. Shock (ed.), *The Liberal Tradition from Fox to Keynes* (A. & C. Black, 1956)— very good documentary exposition. J. A. Thompson, *The Collapse of the British Liberal Party* (D. C. Heath, 1964)—a valuable symposium of contrasting viewpoints. T. Wilson, *The Downfall of the Liberal Party 1914–1935* (Collins, 1966)—an important study. H. Pelling, *A Short History of the Labour Party* (Macmillan, 1961)—the best introduction. P. P. Poirier, *The Advent of the Labour Party* (Allen and Unwin, 1958)— most useful. H. Pelling, *The Origins of the Labour Party* (Macmillan, 1954)—a valuable work. H. Pelling (ed.), *The Challenge of Socialism* (A. & C. Black, 1954)—interesting.

FURTHER READING

Major Issues 1900–1914

R. Jenkins, *Mr. Balfour's Poodle* (Heinemann, 1954)—an indispensable work on the constitutional crisis. M. Bruce, *The Coming of the Welfare State* (Batsford, 1965)—a thorough account. B. B. Gilbert, *The Evolution of National Insurance in Great Britain* (Michael Joseph, 1966)—an authoritative work. R. D. H. Seaman (ed.), *The Liberals and the Welfare State* (E. Arnold, 1968)—some useful extracts. J. C. Beckett, *The Making of Modern Ireland 1603–1923* (Faber and Faber, 1966)—an excellent account. F. S. L. Lyons, *Ireland since the Famine* (Weidenfeld and Nicolson, 1971)—an indispensable guide. N. Mansergh, *The Irish Question 1840–1921* (Allen and Unwin, 1965)—a valuable analysis. A. T. Q. Stewart, *The Ulster Crisis* (Faber and Faber, 1967)—interesting. H. Pelling, *A History of British Trade Unionism* (Macmillan, 1963)—the best introduction. E. H. Phelps Brown, *The Growth of British Industrial Relations* (Macmillan, 1965)—an important work. C. Rover, *Women's Suffrage and Party Politics in Britain 1866–1914* (R.K.P., 1967)—particularly valuable analysis. R. Fulford, *Votes for Women* (Faber and Faber, 1957)—the best account. F. W. Pethick-Lawrence, *Fate has been Kind* (Hutchison, 1943)—valuable. M. G. Fawcett, *The Women's Victory and After* (Sidgwick and Jackson)—interesting. A. J. Marder, *From the Dreadnought to Scapa Flow, I—The Road to War 1904–14* (O.U.P., 1961)—an outstanding and indispensable work of scholarship. R. Hough, *First Sea Lord: Admiral Sir John Fisher* (Allen and Unwin, 1969)—very readable.

Index